WASHOE COUNTY LIBRARY

3 1235 0

P9-BIG-978

SPELL IT
RIGHT!

SPELL IT RIGHT!

FOURTH EDITION

HARRY SHAW

WASHOE COUNTY LIBRARY
RENO, NEVADA

HarperPerennial
A Division of HarperCollins*Publishers*

3 1235 00879 1977

SPELL IT RIGHT! (*Fourth Edition*). Copyright © 1993 by Harry Lee Shaw, Jr. All rights reserved. Printed in the United States of America. No part of this book may be used or reproduced in any manner whatsoever without written permission except in the case of brief quotations embodied in critical articles and reviews. For information address HarperCollins Publishers, 10 East 53rd Street, New York, NY 10022

HarperCollins books may be purchased for educational, business, or sales promotional use. For information, please write: Special Markets Department, HarperCollins Publishers, Inc., 10 East 53rd Street, New York, NY 10022.

FIRST HARPERPERENNIAL EDITION

Library of Congress Cataloging-in-Publication Data

Shaw, Harry, 1905 –
    Spell it right! / Harry Shaw. — 4th ed.
        p.   cm.
    Includes index.
    ISBN 0-06-461046-2
    1. English language—Orthography and spelling.   I. Title.
PE1143.S48   1993
428.1—dc20   92-11518

421.52

92 93 94 95 96   PS/CW   10 9 8 7 6 5 4 3 2 1

CONTENTS

FOREWORD

Correct spelling is essential for intelligent communication. It is taken for granted and expected at all times. Yet many people realize their writing sometimes contains spelling errors, and they are embarrassed by doubts and fears about the correct spelling of difficult words. Distraction, confusion, and misunderstanding result from errors in spelling. Therefore, no one should be satisfied with anything less than perfection.

Perhaps you are one of those people who feel disturbed by their spelling errors and have enough of a spelling conscience to do something about it. Or perhaps you are among those who doubt their ability to master this difficult subject. You may have tried many times and failed. If so, is there any hope for you?

The answer is that if you really have a desire to learn to spell perfectly you can, provided:

1. You can pronounce such words as *accept* and *except* so that they will not sound exactly alike.
2. You can look at such words as *sad* and *sand* and in a single glance, without moving your eyes, detect the difference between them.
3. You can sign your name without looking at the paper on which you are writing and without even consciously thinking about what you are doing.
4. You can tell your friend Bill from your friend Sam by a mere glance.

5. You can learn a simple rhyme, such as "Old King Cole was a merry old soul . . ."
6. You can remember that a compliment is "what *I* like to get."
7. You can learn the alphabet, if you do not know it already.
8. You can equip yourself with a reliable desk dictionary.

SPELL IT RIGHT!

1

YOU AND THE PROBLEM
OF SPELLING

The one thing demanded of those who have had educational advantages is that they be able to spell. In your daily work or in social situations you may not need to be able to add a column of figures. Few people will care. Not often will you be thought stupid if you don't know the dates of historical events—say, the Battle of Waterloo. Your knowledge of economics can be nil. You may not know the difference between an oboe and an ibis, an atom and a molecule. But if you can't spell, you're in trouble. Rightly or wrongly, fairly or unfairly, misspelling is the most frequently accepted sign of illiteracy.

Why is this? You can argue that the ability to think clearly is far more important than spelling. So are clear expression of thoughts, an attractive personality, and demonstrated ability in one's job. The fact remains that incorrect spelling is heavily penalized in our society—so heavily that it keeps people from getting jobs they want or prevents them from moving up to better positions. Inability to spell gives people complexes just as much as unsureness about grammar or proper methods of dress and social behavior.

Why Correct Spelling Is Important

Job opportunities are missed and employees are often let go because of spelling deficiencies. Even business enterprises can suffer because of their inability to meet commonly accepted spelling practices. In an eastern city a store was opened for the sale of

Army surplus goods: canteens, combat boots, pup tents, plastic boxes, and various other items. Over the door was a sign that said COME IN AND BROUSE AROUND. One day somebody told the owner that BROUSE was a misspelling. So he had it painted this way: COME IN AND BROWZE AROUND. Another customer complained and the owner got another repainting: COME IN AND BROWS AROUND. There must have been more complaints, because a few days later a new sign appeared that read: COME IN AND BROUSE, BROWZE OR BROWS AROUND—BUT COME IN. A month or so later, the owner tacked up another sign over that one. It read: GOING OUT OF BIZNESS.

The main reason for reliance on spelling as an index of intelligence and literacy is that correct spelling is the one fixed and certain thing about our language. The overwhelming majority of English words are spelled in only one way; all other ways are wrong. The accepted system *is* accepted. It is the system in which our business communications, our magazines, our newspapers, and our books have been written for generations.

The uniformity applies to no other aspect of our language. You can vary your choice of words as much as you please. You can write sentences which are long or short and punctuate them in various ways. In most circles you can split an infinitive or use a double negative and not be penalized. But you can spell a word in only one correct way. In a rapidly changing world this substantial uniformity is understandably attractive to many people, particularly to those who are good spellers.

Even where alternative spellings are possible, only one will be thought correct for a given piece of writing. For example, both *telephone* and *phone* are commonly used, the latter a colloquial form of *telephone*. Your employer may insist on *telephone*, and that full spelling will then be the right one. Both *theater* and *theatre* are correct spellings, but you would probably use the former in the United States and the latter in England.

One might argue logically that many wrong spellings are "better" than the right ones since they "show" the word more clearly. *Wensday* more clearly reveals the sound of the word than does *Wednesday*. But logic and common sense will not help; in Old English *Wödnes daeg* was the day of the god Woden, and the *d* has remained. Spelling is frequently a matter of conforming not to logic but to custom and tradition.

If enough people make a "mistake" in punctuation, or grammar, or the meaning of a word, that "mistake" becomes acceptable usage. This is a scientific fact of language. Through the years our language has changed, and will change, in its idioms, its vocabulary, its pronunciation, and its structural form. Change is the essential, inevitable phenomenon of a living language, as it is of any living organism. But this observation, this law, does not yet apply to the spelling of English words.

For many generations, spelling practice has been supported by sentiment, convention, prejudice, and custom. This is strong support, since each of us can think of many other activities similarly reinforced. The world is largely ruled by sentiment. A hundred, a thousand, observances are based only upon convention. Think briefly of the clothes people wear, table manners, office etiquette, and you will see the point. If sentiment, convention, and custom were removed from our social order, our way of living would be altered beyond recognition.

If English spelling were much more illogical than it is, the problem might be solved. Then no one could spell correctly; all of us would be bad spellers together. But enough people have learned to spell correctly to make things difficult for those who can't. This is the situation today, and we must make the best of it.

At some time in the distant future, correct spelling may be thought unimportant. Until that time, we can take comfort in realizing that spelling, like every other activity of the human mind, *can* be learned. It will have to be if we are to free ourselves from the doubts and frustrations which diminish our self-confidence when we write. It will have to be if we wish to "get ahead," to be socially acceptable, to be considered educated and literate.

Why Spelling Is Difficult

Correct spelling is so important for social and business reasons that we feel obligated to learn to spell as well as we can, perfectly if possible. The task is not simple. It would be easier if spelling were always logical and consistent. But from bitter experience we know that the spelling of English words is illogical and inconsistent. In fact, it is downright eccentric and, on occasion, idiotic— as writers through the years have gleefully, or wrathfully, pointed out. Thorstein Veblen, famed author of *The Theory of the Leisure Class*, once wrote that English spelling satisfies all the requirements "of conspicuous waste. It is archaic, cumbrous, and ineffective . . . failure to acquire it is easy of detection . . ." as many of us know to our sorrow. And former President Andrew Jackson once angrily commented that it is a poor mind that cannot think of more than one way to spell a word.

Why is spelling difficult? The primary reason is that the correct spelling of many words does not even approximate the sounds being represented. The forty-odd sounds of our speech are represented with an alphabet of only twenty-six letters. Of these, only three are really active because *c* (or *k*), *g*, and *x* duplicate the work of other letters. The twenty-three active letters alone or in combinations like *sh* and *ea* are required to represent more than forty distinctive sounds. For example, the vowel *a* spells the vowel sounds of *far, fare, lay, lap,* and *many.*

However, the limitations of the alphabet could be overcome if pronunciation didn't constantly keep changing. Years ago English spelling tradition was established and was stabilized by sixteenth- and seventeenth-century printers. Over the centuries the pronunciation of many words has changed, but spelling has not. Unless spelling undergoes reform (and strong opposition has always prevented this), our spelling may proceed to the point where many words become ideographic. This means that a written symbol (a spelled word) will represent something directly rather than stand for the actual sound of the word itself (as in Chinese). This tendency—exemplified by the contrasting pronunciation and spelling of such words as *cough, knife,* and *Worcester*—has been evident for centuries. This difference will probably become greater and greater as time goes on.

The English habit of borrowing words from other languages is responsible for such groups of words as *fine* and *sign; site* and *sight; no* and *know.* Our borrowing habit has brought in thousands of words that do not follow English spelling conventions—*khaki, croquet, bureau.* No one unfamiliar with English and English spelling would ever imagine that *kernel* and *colonel* have the same sound.

Another problem arises from our continuing spellings that were significant in another language, such as the Latin endings *-ance, -ence* and *-able, -ible.* Each of these pairs is now pronounced the same and has the same general meaning so that it is not easy to remember which one is required in a particular word.

English spelling cannot really be defended. But its confusion and the form of a particular word can be clarified somewhat by reference to the history of English spelling.

A Brief History of English Spelling

No adequate history of English spelling has ever been written, and certainly this small book is not the place to attempt one. But a brief review of known facts about our language will help to account for some of the admitted difficulties of English spelling.

For about one thousand years before the Christian era, our linguistic ancestors were semi-savages wandering through northern Europe. These tribes consisted of Angles, Saxons, and Jutes and spoke several dialects of what is known as Low German, or *Plattdeutsch.* They had some contact with the Roman Empire and promptly began a process which has continued unabated to the present day: they started borrowing words from Latin and placing them in their own vocabularies. We still use many everyday words borrowed by these tribes, such as: *bishop, butter, cheap, cheese, church, plum, kettle, street.*

When the Roman Empire began to weaken, it had to give up its occupancy of what we now know as England, and the Germanic tribes, commonly called Anglo-Saxons, began to move in. We know little about the arrival of the Anglo-Saxons in England in the fifth century A.D., but we do know that after the year 600 they were converted to Christianity and that borrowing from Latin became even more pronounced. To what was then Anglo-Saxon, or Old English, were added many words which are in use today, such as *alms, anthem, martyr, palm,* and *priest.*

England even then was considered an attractive place, and

Norsemen from Denmark and the Scandinavian peninsula began a long series of hit-and-run raids. Forays of the Norsemen continued until the eleventh century, with the linguistic result that many Norse words were added to the language. Examples are *crawl, egg, law, race, scowl,* and *tree.* Even our pronouns *they, them,* and *their* are of Norse origin. So is our suffix *-by,* the Danish word for "farm" or "town," which appears in so many place names, such as *Derby.*

Another event of great importance to our language (and spelling) was the Norman Conquest. The Normans, originally from Scandinavia, settled in northern France in the tenth century and adopted the French language. In 1066 they crossed the English Channel and became the masters of England. French became the language of the nobility, the court, and polite society, although the common people continued to use English. Our language was profoundly affected by the introduction of French; literally thousands of words were added to the English vocabulary between 1100 and 1500. A few examples will serve to show this borrowing: *bacon, baptism, biscuit, blanket, bucket, chess, curtain, fault, flower, government, grammar, incense, lamp, lemon, logic, parson, religion, scarlet, surprise, towel.*

Beginning about 1500, the discovery of new lands brought many thousands of other new words to the English language. Words from such remote regions as India, China, Africa, and North America enriched the language tremendously. Among familiar words borrowed, for example, from the North American Indians may be mentioned *Connecticut, Massachusetts, Monongahela, squaw, tomahawk,* and *wampum.*

In short, during the past thousand years our language has far more than doubled its size. Words have come pouring into the language from French, Latin, Greek, Hebrew, Arabic, and a score of other tongues. Many of these words are difficult to spell, at least in part because of their pronunciation.

This brief comment on English is grossly inadequate as linguistic history, but its purpose is to make clear one dominant reason why spelling and pronunciation are so far apart. When these many thousands of words first arrived in English they often appeared with the spellings, or phonetic (sound) approximations of the spellings, which they originally had and which did not always conform to the customs of English. Sometimes, the spellings of words were modified to conform to the English tongue; many times they were not. The English language is a linguistic grab bag with tremendous range and flexibility. Unfortunately, its very richness compounds our spelling problems.

English is indeed a polyglot language, but that is not all. Present-day spelling often reflects pronunciations of several centuries ago. Between the time of Chaucer (*ca* 1342–1400) and Shakespeare (1564–1616) our language underwent changes in pronunciation which contributed to the chaos of modern spelling.

For example, in Chaucer's time *mouse* sounded like our *moose; moon* resembled our pronunciation of *moan*. These shifts in vowel sounds (as well as in others) were thorough. However, since we have retained some of the Chaucerian (Middle English) system of spelling, Modern and Chaucerian English seem closer than they really are. Genuine differences are hidden by our spelling system.

Another change during this period from Chaucer to Shakespeare was the complete elimination of a vowel sound in certain positions. Chaucer pronounced *name* and *dance* as two syllables. Shakespeare pronounced them as one, as do we. Similarly, Chaucer pronounced the word *laughed* as two syllables: laugh-ed, but of course we do not. This elimination of a vowel sound affected hundreds of quite common words and gave a different aspect to the language. The "silent" vowel in English is responsible for as many misspellings as any other one cause (it will be discussed in Chapter 4).

These two changes in pronunciation (but not in spelling) account for some of the basic differences between the English of Chaucer's time and that of today. Furthermore, a number of other sound changes have occurred since the time of Shakespeare and are still going on. People in the sixteenth and seventeenth centuries, for example, pronounced *reason* as we do *raisin*. They also sounded the *l* in a word like *palm*. Our pronunciation has changed, but our spelling has not—with consequent grief for all poor spellers.

Why is it that pronunciation is ever changing and spelling is not? Many reasons can be cited, but two are outstanding.

First, standardization of spelling is due more to the invention of printing than to any other single cause. Prior to the introduction of printing into England by William Caxton in 1475, most people were not concerned with spelling. Reading and writing were activities carried on only by monks and other learned men. So long as people communicated solely by speech, spelling was no problem. But when printing came in, some standards had to be set up; otherwise, chaos would have resulted because those who read would have been utterly confused by whimsically varied spelling. As larger and larger numbers of people began to read and write, they saw and used the standardized spellings employed by scholars, "editors," and printers. These standards were loose and flexible, to be sure, but they represented a forward step in communication. This unification of the language, though partial and imperfect, had a profound effect on writing but not, of course, on speech.

Second, a major regulatory and controlling influence on the language came from early dictionary-makers. The first English dictionary in 1603 spelled and briefly defined a little more than two thousand words. Its compiler did what his predecessors had done when translating Latin words into English: he copied. Naturally, on numerous occasions he imitated the spellings of his predecessors and thus tended to freeze them.

The earliest dictionary was imitated, or expanded upon, by several other lexicographers. In 1755, Dr. Samuel Johnson published his famous dictionary, a serious, important work that has influenced all lexicographers ever since. His dictionary dominated—and tended to fix—English spelling and usage for more than a century.

In the United States the great pioneer in dictionary-making was Noah Webster. His first work, published in 1806, advocated spelling *head* as *hed* and *thumb* as *thum*, but his efforts at spelling reform were generally rejected by the public. In other respects, however, his work was widely accepted; and in 1828 his *An American Dictionary of the English Language* began to exert its lasting influence on English in this country. Lexicographers since Webster have been somewhat more reliable than he in reporting actual usage but they, too, have had to report spelling as it is found in printed sources. Thus, spelling has become fixed and largely unchangeable, although it frequently does not represent actual pronunciation and often departs from common sense.

Some Comforting Thoughts About Spelling

If you have read this far, you may have become discouraged about ever learning to spell correctly. You may say, and with reason, that such a weird and illogical system deserves not study but contempt. Nevertheless, you know from experience that powerful social and business considerations force you to master the subject. Actually, the problem is not so difficult to solve as it may seem.

In the first place, psychologists and experienced educators have proved over and over again that any person of normal intelligence can learn to spell. Like any other activity of the human mind, spelling can be approached, grasped, and mastered. It is easier for some people to spell correctly than it is for others. This is understandable; some people can master calculus or ice-skating or sewing or typing or reading more easily than others. Spelling correctly may not be simple for you, but it surely cannot be termed impossible. Hundreds of thousands of "bad" spellers have conquered their difficulties. So can you, if you really desire to and will apply yourself to the task. No special quality of mind, no rare set of mental or motor reflexes, is involved.

It is true, however, that minds work in different ways. The best and easiest way for John or Mary to learn to spell correctly may not be the most efficient for George or Abigail. But one or more of the six approaches discussed in this book will help John, Mary, George, Abigail—and you. What you need is the will, the desire, to learn. Having that, and normal intelligence, you are fully equipped. One commentator on spelling has flatly stated: "All the investigations indicate that any *child* of normal intelligence can learn to spell with very little difficulty in a reasonable length of time."

A second comforting thought about spelling is that probably only a few words cause most of the trouble. Learning to spell may seem a hopeless task because so many thousands of words must be mastered. But remember that no one is expected to be able to spell every word on demand. A physician might be able to spell *sphygmomanometer*, but nearly everyone else would have to look it up in a dictionary. And since physicians are no better spellers than any other group of educated people, they, like us, would properly consult a dictionary when writing such "demons" as *piccalilli, platyrrhine,* and *pseudepigrapha.* (These words may seem strange because many of us have never used them in our entire lives. Yet each appears in standard desk dictionaries.)

We use remarkably few different words in ordinary speech, and the overwhelming majority of them cause no problems whatever. It may be both startling and reassuring to learn that only twelve simple words account for about 25 percent of everything spoken and written in English. The dozen most used words in English are *a, and, he, I, in, it, is, of, that, the, to,* and *was.* These twelve and thirty-eight more (a total of fifty words) make up half of the running total in all English speech and writing. If you increase the number to the thousand most common words in English, you will account for 80 percent of all words everyone uses in speaking and writing and comes across in reading.

You may be inclined to doubt these statements, but they are substantiated by the word count contained in *The Teacher's Word Book of 30,000 Words,* prepared under the direction of two outstanding scholars, Edward L. Thorndike and Irving Lorge. Other experts unhesitatingly accept the findings of Thorndike and Lorge.

If only one thousand different words appear in some 80 percent of all the expressions that one says, hears, writes, and reads, it follows that the task of learning to spell that small number should be simple. And yet the problem is even more elementary: almost none of the thousand words creates any spelling difficulty whatever for the ordinary writer.

In a running count of many millions of words used by speakers and writers of English, the words *a, and, of, the,* and *to* will appear more than a hundred thousand times; *he, I, in, it, is, that,* and *was* will appear more than fifty thousand times. None of these words is a spelling demon, nor indeed are many of the 620 words appearing more than one thousand times in the same word count.

For proof of this statement, note the thirty-nine most often used words beginning with the letter *a:*

a	all	answer
about	almost	any
according	alone	anything
across	along	appear
act	already	are
action	also	arm
add	always	army
after	am	around
afternoon	American	art
again	among	as
against	an	ask
age	and	at
ago	another	away

Do you find any hard-to-spell words in this list? And just so that you will not think the list is rigged with words starting with *a*, see whether the *u* words are any more difficult:

uncle	United States	upon
under	until	us
understand	up	use

You can come to terms with the spelling problem if you will narrow your sights and concentrate on the few, but very real, troublemakers. When driving a car haven't you often noticed in the distance a hill which looked very steep, the road up it almost vertical? As you got closer, the road seemed to smooth out, didn't it? What seemed an impossibly sharp climb became a simple grade. Learning to spell involves climbing a grade, but not a very steep one, once you get close to the problem.

Another reassuring thought about learning to spell is that the task can become good fun and provide much pleasure. This statement may seem absurd, but it is an acknowledged fact of human behavior that the more proficient a person becomes in some activity, the greater his pleasure in it. Ever watch a figure skater?

Two boys with a baseball? A woman knitting? A mother giving her child a bath? Two chess players? Someone lost in a book?

Learning to spell involves discipline, concentration, and some hard work. But so do figure-skating, baseball, knitting, and reading. Proficiency provides pleasure in these activities; often the more skill attained, the greater the pleasure. Further, most activities can best be learned by actually participating in them, not just memorizing rules or reading about them in books or magazines.

After you have attained greater proficiency in spelling by following the suggestions in this book, you will find word games enjoyable. Crossword puzzles and cryptograms are not recommended for the initial phases of spelling study. Yet they can, and do, provide pleasure for many people and unquestionably increase one's basic vocabulary and spelling proficiency. Many average spellers have become excellent ones through games like Scrabble and anagrams. Only a few decades ago, spelling bees were commonly held in almost every grade school in the country. They provided fun and excitement for those who participated, as some of my readers can testify. National spelling bees are still an annual occurrence. Perhaps some television program will revive the old-time spelling bee, with pleasure and profit for contestants and viewers.

Recently, my wife and I had dinner with another couple. After returning to the living room, our host suggested that instead of playing bridge or engaging in small talk, we try a spelling game. Each of us wrote down on paper three words which we thought would cause spelling difficulties for the others. We read out our lists in turn and the others wrote them down. When each of us had written the twelve words, we read out the spellings and settled arguments by using a dictionary. Result: we added some new words to our vocabularies, fixed their spellings in mind, and enjoyed ourselves immensely. You might like to know a few of the "demons" used that night. Here they are: *picnicking, phthisic, deciduous, gnat, medieval, ptomaine, dahlia, garrulous, tendency, picayune, ecstasy, liquefy, battalion, dilemma, obsession, amoeba, iridescent, supercilious.*

Several of these words are of little practical value. That's not the point. What is important is that four people of ordinary intelligence derived pleasure and profit from a "dull" spelling game.

Learning to spell well is not a matter of tricks and mirrors; it is not a dull and dreary chore; it is not an unending task which stretches out indefinitely. It is a subject that can be mastered with some effort and imagination—and a common-sense approach.

2

TACKLING THE PROBLEM

Nearly every spelling authority who has written on the subject has presented some sure-fire approach to the problem of poor spelling. All other methods are wrong; his is the only true one. And his method *has* worked—for some people. For others it has been a flat failure. There was nothing especially wrong with his method except that it did not allow for the fact that people differ. They differ in sex, color, and personality—and they differ in ways of learning. The system by which A learns easily and quickly may work poorly for B or may not work at all. There is no one guaranteed method for everyone, but some plans for studying spelling are sounder than others. Actually, spelling is sometimes "taught" in such a fashion as to preclude any possibility of real success. Before explaining the six approaches recommended in this book, we should review a few facts about people and the learning process.

Our minds operate in accordance with certain principles. We may call them *laws* if we wish, although reputable experimental psychologists would hardly do so. For instance, you have probably long since found out that you can remember something which is important to you. You can remember it so well, so clearly, that you think you could never forget it. You also realize that you can conveniently fail to remember things you wish to forget—dental appointments, for example.

Incentive, then, or a strong motive to remember, will facilitate memory. And a good memory will aid the process of learning.

14

Thus, the task of learning to spell will come easier to you if you bear in mind the practical value to be gained and discipline yourself to study and practice.

Forming Mental Images

The mental process most important in word study is the ability to form mental pictures, or *mental images* as they may be called. These images are of several types. For example, each of us can form some sort of visual image when a suggested idea calls up in our minds a picture. When the word *church* is suggested to you, you immediately "see in your mind" a picture of the object named. So do I, although your visual image and mine may differ. Almost any object—automobile, child, office manager, snow—will summon up for you, and for everyone, some sort of visual image.

This power of visualization is far stronger in some people than in others. You may know every detail about your bedroom and yet not be able to see it in your mind's eye. Many of us have lapses in our powers of visualization. Therefore, the suggestion set forth later, that you "mentally see" words, may or may not be helpful to you. If it isn't, some other approach will make more sense. It's no discredit not to have visual memory, although it is true that this mental process can be trained. You probably can close your eyes and, without difficulty, see your own signature. But you may not be able to "see" any of the words you persistently misspell. If so, try another approach.

Auditory Images

When a suggested idea summons up a memory of what the object sounds like, we have an *auditory* (hearing) image. Some of us can, and some cannot, "mentally hear" the sounds named in "the bark of a gun," "the popping of hot fat," "the song of a lark," "the laughter of children." Being auditory-minded is not especially helpful in learning to spell, unless we are also visual-minded. If we are both, the sounds of a few words can be compared with their visual images. Some of the memory devices (*mnemonics*) suggested later (Chapter 16) depend upon this relationship.

Motor Images

Related to the visual image and the auditory image is the *motor* image. Motor images are connected with the use of different muscles in the body. If you are a swimmer and think of the last lap in a long race, you can summon up the feeling of weary arm and leg muscles.

How can a motor image apply to spelling? Have you ever said of the spelling of a word you have in mind: "That may not be correct. Wait until I write it"? If so, you have called upon a motor image (hand-motor memory) to aid your visual memory. Motor memory is, for some people, a powerful aid in spelling; they apparently can actually feel the motions called into play by writing. You can close your eyes and without conscious thought write your signature entirely from "feel": this is motor memory.

The more mental images you have of words, the better your spelling will become. Visual, auditory, and motor images can aid in recalling correct spellings. This fundamental principle of the human mental process has an enormously important bearing on learning to spell and explains why some methods are ineffective and wasteful. For one example, you may have tried to learn the spelling of some word by repeating its letters to yourself over and over. If you have an especially well-developed "auditory memory," this method may work. But auditory images are difficult or impossible for many people to summon up. In fact, some psychologists maintain it is the least developed means of recall for most of us. Mouthing words over and over is a complete waste of time for a majority of people.

When you were in school and misspelled a word, your teacher may have required you to write it correctly ten, twenty, or a hundred times. Such drill was designed to fix the word so firmly in your motor memory that you would never misspell it again. Unfortunately, such drill can, and often does, become rote; you perform the exercise without conscious attention to what you're doing. You are expending muscular effort but not relating it to visual or auditory images. We all realize that we perform certain acts with little or no conscious attention so that we are hardly aware of the process involved: shifting automobile gears, sewing, walking, carrying food to our mouths with a fork, even reading. But learning to spell requires attention and concentration, not rote methods that have little or no relationship to forming important mental images.

Six Paths to Correct Spelling

Learning to spell is an individual matter. What works for you may not work for your friend, and vice versa. (It's even possible, but not likely, that some people can learn to spell words by mouthing them or writing them down a hundred times.) But there are a half-dozen approaches which may be effective. One or more may work for you, depending upon your mental make-up. Almost surely, one method will be better than others for you.

My suggestion is that you select a small group of words whose spelling causes you difficulty. Try studying them in turn by the methods mentioned below and developed in succeeding chapters. It should be fairly simple to decide which approach works best for you—that is, which is quickest, surest, and has the longest lasting effects.

These six methods, discussed fully in chapters which follow, have worked for millions of people. Each is psychologically sound; each has individual merits. But not all of them will work for you. If you can't "visualize" words (the most helpful approach for the largest number of people), don't lose heart; one of the other methods may suit your individual mental processes far better. Here, then, are the six methods:

1. **Actually see words as well as hear them.**
2. **Pronounce words carefully and correctly.**
3. **Use a dictionary.**
4. **Learn a few simple rules of spelling.**
5. **Spell carefully.**
6. **Use memory devices.**

3

ACTUALLY SEE WORDS
AS WELL AS HEAR THEM

As was pointed out in Chapter 2, visual memory is part of everyone's mental equipment. It is better developed in some people than in others, but each of us has at least a trace. Otherwise, we could hardly recognize a sight or a person previously noticed with only casual observation. You do not need to undertake a feature-by-feature examination to distinguish George from Sam: you know instantly, from visual memory, which friend is which. No matter how poorly developed, your visual memory is a storehouse of familiar images.

The ability to visualize words, to see them in the mind's eye, is the hallmark of the good speller. To mix some metaphors, it is his "ace in the hole," his "secret weapon." When a word is mentioned, a proficient speller can "see" the word in full detail, every letter standing out, as though it were written on paper, or the floor, the wall, the sky—against whatever background object he calls to mind. If you are a poor speller, you lack this ability to some degree. Why is this so?

Perhaps one reason is that you learned to read words as units and were not required to sound them out letter-by-letter and syllable-by-syllable. Such a method of teaching was partly a protest against the chaotic or nonexistent relationship between sound and symbol in many English words. This approach also recognized that we *do* read words as units, not as successions of letters. Possibly this "modern" method of teaching reading helped to create many poor spellers.

It is quite possible to learn the general appearance of words on flash cards and later to recognize them elsewhere. You have no difficulty in visualizing such words as *cat*, *hat*, *dog*, and *run*. But unless you have actually studied them, you may mistake *their* for *there*, or *its* for *it's*, to mention only two examples of oft-misspelled words. (Fortunately, most teachers have long since modified this new approach and now teach not only by word units but also by sounds, letters, and syllables.)

Your Perception Span

Again, your difficulty in visualizing words may have to do with your perception span. Some people can form a remarkably definite and complete impression of an entire room at a single glance; others can look at the same room for minutes on end without really "seeing" it at all. Similarly, many words contain too many letters for some people to take in at a single glance; possibly three to five letters is all they can perceive at one time. (Please remember that we are here discussing not reading but accurate and detailed mental pictures.)

If your ability to "see words in your mind" is weak and faulty, begin by dividing the words you are studying into syllables. Then you can focus on one syllable at a time (usually two to five letters) and not stretch your perception (seeing) span beyond reasonable limits. After learning to "see" each syllable separately, you can more and more easily visualize the complete word made up of separately seen units. For example, if you cannot mentally see the word *compete*, focus first on *com* and then on *pete*. When you have learned to see each unit, you can readily see them combined. If you cannot "see" the word *competitively*, try focusing on each of the individual units and then combine them: *com-pet-i-tive-ly.*

A principle of photography may be of help with this problem. What we call a snapshot is an instantaneous photograph—a picture taken with a small amount of exposure time. Other pictures require longer exposure for varying reasons. Simple words like *cat*, *dog*, *boy*, and *am* may be called snapshots—they make an instantaneous clear image on the mind. But words like *cataclysm*, *dogged, boycott,* and *amphibious* require longer exposure. That is, you must look at them, probably by syllables, long enough to form clear and precise mental images of them.

When you have a strong, completely established mental picture of a word, you can spell it on any occasion without hesitation or difficulty. The greatest single mistake of the poor speller is not looking at a word with enough care and time to fix it in his mind firmly and forever. Don't say that you can't do this; you already have done so with many words. You can picture and spell without hesitation many simple and even some very complex words. You can do this for your own name, for your town or city, and for the street on which you live. That is, you have looked at these words and have actually *seen* what you looked at.

How to "See" Words Mentally

Here is a good method of learning to "see" words mentally:

1. With your eyes on the word being studied, pronounce it carefully. If you don't know the proper pronunciation, consult a dictionary.
2. Study each individual letter in the word; if the word has more than one syllable, separate the syllables and focus on each one in turn.
3. *Close your eyes* and pronounce and spell the word either letter-by-letter or syllable-by-syllable, depending upon its length.
4. Look at the word again to make certain that you have recalled it correctly.
5. Practice this alternate fixing of the image and its recall until you are certain that you can instantly "see" the word under any circumstances and at any time.

Such a procedure is especially valuable when dealing with tricky words which add or drop letters for no apparent reason; which contain silent letters; or which transpose or change letters without logical cause:

explain but *explanation*	*curious* but *curiosity*
proceed but *procedure*	*maintain* but *maintenance*
pronounce but *pronunciation*	*fire* but *fiery*

The most frequent error in visualizing words is mistaking one for another similar to it. A *homograph* is a word identical with another and therefore causes no spelling trouble, whatever difficulty it may provide in pronunciation and correct usage. The *bow* in *bow tie* is spelled the same as the word *bow*, meaning "to bend," but differs in pronunciation and meaning.

Homonyms, however, do cause spelling trouble. They are words identical in pronunciation but with different meanings and often with different spellings. If you spell *bore* when you mean *boar*, or *meet* when you mean *meat*, you have incurred homonym trouble. The only sure remedy for this type of blunder is to study such words until they and their meanings are fixed in your mind.

You should understand the meanings of each of the following words and not use one when you mean another. If you will concentrate on each individual word and its meaning as suggested in the five steps on page 20, you should be able to bring it to mind whenever you have occasion to use it. The words in each group in the following list resemble each other in some way, although many of them are neither homonyms nor homographs. Carefully "seeing" them will remove your spelling problems with this class of words. Pronunciation is still another matter; not all of the grouped words which follow are pronounced identically, but all those in one group do have some resemblance to each other.

This list is far from complete. Hundreds of additional words could have been included, but those given here are the ones most often confused. Also, please remember that some of the words which follow have more than one part of speech. Usually, only one part of speech is indicated, since we are concentrating on spelling rather than grammar. Again, not all meanings are provided for every word. Consult your dictionary if you need further information about variant meanings of the words and word groups which follow.

Look-Alikes and Sound-Alikes

1. **Accede**—To agree or consent. I *accede* to your request.
   Exceed—To surpass. Don't *exceed* the speed limit.
2. **Accent**—Emphasis in speaking. Put more *accent* on the first syllable.
   Ascent—A rising, a going up. The path has a steep *ascent*.
   Assent—Consent, agreement. The proposal easily won our *assent*.
3. **Accept**—To receive. Joan would not *accept* the gift.
   Except—To omit or exempt. The soldier was *excepted* from guard duty that day.
4. **Access**—Admittance, way or approach. He has *access* to the vaults.
   Excess—Surpassing limits. The meeting was marked by an *excess* of good feeling.
5. **Adapt**—To change, make suitable. He *adapted* himself to the new plan.
   Adept—Skilled, expert. Joan was *adept* in cooking.
   Adopt—To choose, select. I shall *adopt* your proposal.
6. **Adverse**—Hostile, opposed. George had an *adverse* opinion.
   Averse—Unwilling, reluctant. He was *averse* to joining us.
7. **Advice**—Counsel (a noun). Please accept my *advice*.
   Advise—To give counsel (a verb). I *advise* you to go.
8. **Affect**—To influence, produce change. Your plan *affects* my purpose.
   Effect—Result, change. What will be the *effect* of your decision?
9. **Air**—Mixture of gases. He likes to breathe fresh *air*.
   Heir—One who inherits. She was my daughter and only *heir*.
10. **Aisle**—Passageway, corridor. Mary walked slowly down the *aisle*.

Isle—Land surrounded by water. He wants to live on a deserted *isle*.

11. **Alimentary**—Connected with food, nutrition. The surgeon removed an obstruction in Sue's *alimentary* canal.

    Elementary—Connected with rudiments, fundamentals. The little boy has just started *elementary* school.

12. **Allay**—To rest, to relieve. Medicine will *allay* your pain.

    Alley—Narrow passage. This *alley* leads nowhere.

    Alleys—Narrow passages (plural). The city has many blind *alleys*.

    Allies—Partners, comrades (plural). The *Allies* defeated Germany.

    Ally—To join with (verb), one who joins (noun). Please *ally* yourself with our campaign. England has often been an *ally* of the United States.

13. **All ready**—All are ready. We'll leave when we are *all ready*.

    Already—Earlier, previously. When we arrived, Bill had *already* left.

14. **All together**—All in company. The family was *all together* for the event.

    Altogether—Wholly, completely. He was not *altogether* pleased by the outcome of the election.

15. **Allude**—To make reference to. The speaker *alluded* to the bad record of his opponents.

    Elude—To escape, to evade. Big money has always *eluded* my group of friends.

16. **Allusion**—A reference to (noun). He made an *allusion* to those not present.

    Illusion—Deception (noun). This is an optical *illusion*.

17. **Altar**—Place of worship (noun). Many knelt at the *altar*.

    Alter—To change (verb). Do not *alter* your scheme.

18. **Always**—Continually, forever. I shall *always* love Joy.

    All ways—Without exception. He is prepared in *all ways* to do the job.

19. **Amateur**—Nonprofessional. He is an *amateur* chef.
    Armature—Armorlike covering. The *armature* of this dynamo needs repair.

20. **An**—One, each. This is *an* excellent report.
    And—Also, plus. He ate a peach *and* a pear.

21. **Angel**—Celestial being. You are far from being an *angel*.
    Angle—Geometric figure. The *angle* of the street was sharp.

22. **Ante-** —Prefix meaning "before," "prior." She waited in the dentist's *anteroom*.
    Anti- —Prefix meaning "opposite," "against." Iodine is an effective *antiseptic*.

23. **Appraise**—To judge, to estimate. The diamond was *appraised* at one carat.
    Apprise—To inform, notify. We *apprised* him of his election.

24. **Are**—Form of the verb "to be." We *are* ready to eat.
    Or—Conjunction suggesting an alternative. Pay the price *or* walk out.
    Our—Form of the pronoun "we." This is *our* job.

25. **Assay**—A test or to test. He began to *assay* the mineral.
    Essay—An attempt or to try. He *essayed* the difficult job.

26. **Assure**—To convince, to guarantee. I *assured* him of my good will.
    Insure—To secure. He *insured* his house against fire.

27. **Attendance**—An attending, meeting. The *attendance* was greater than expected.
    Attendants—Persons present. The bride had nine *attendants*.

28. **Aught**—Any little part, any respect. For *aught* I know, you are correct.
    Ought—Indicating duty, obligation. Every citizen *ought* to vote.
    Naught—Nothing, zero. Our efforts availed *naught*.

29. **Bail**—Deposited credit. The accused was free on *bail*.
    Bale—Package or bundle. The stevedores hauled *bales* of cotton from the ship.
30. **Baited**—Holding bait. My fishhook was then *baited*.
    Bated—Held in. We watched with *bated* breath.
31. **Ball**—Round object. Nan threw the *ball* to me.
    Bole—Tree trunk. The *bole* was twenty inches in diameter.
    Boll—Pod of a plant. This is a cotton *boll*.
    Bowl—A receptacle (noun) or to roll (verb). This is a china *bowl*. He likes to *bowl* every night.
32. **Baring**—Uncovering. There he stood, *baring* his head to the rain.
    Barring—Excepting. *Barring* the captain, everyone was in the lifeboat.
    Bearing—Carrying, enduring. He is *bearing* up under grave difficulties.
33. **Bazaar**—Market, shop. The church had a *bazaar* to raise money for the altar.
    Bizarre—Odd, queer. The clown's appearance was *bizarre*.
34. **Beach**—Sandy shore, strand. Atlantic City has a famous *beach*.
    Beech—Tree. Peel the bark from that *beech*.
35. **Bear**—To carry (verb) or mammal (noun). People must *bear* their burdens. There is a *bear* in the zoo.
    Bare—Uncovered, empty. This is a *bare* room.
36. **Beat**—To hit or to strike. He *beat* the rug to clean it.
    Beet—A plant. The *beet* is a source of sugar.
37. **Berry**—Fruit. This is a small, juicy *berry*.
    Bury—To preserve, conceal. Please *bury* the evidence.
38. **Berth**—Place to sleep. Henry slept in a lower *berth*.
    Birth—Act of being born. His *birth* occurred in 1930.
39. **Biding**—Waiting, expecting. The nominee was *biding* his time.

Bidding—Command, summons (noun). The *bidding* for property was brisk.

40. **Blew**—Past tense of "blow." The wind *blew* hard.
Blue—Color. He wore a *blue* shirt.

41. **Bloc**—Group of people. They formed a solid *bloc* in the campaign.
Block—A solid (noun) or to impede (verb). This is a heavy *block* of stone. Don't try to *block* this action.

42. **Boar**—Male hog. He shot a splendid wild *boar.*
Bore—To drill or dig. He thinks we should *bore* for water at this place.

43. **Board**—Flat piece of wood. The *board* was heavy.
Bored—Wearied. He was *bored* by the meeting.

44. **Boarder**—Lodger. Mr. Jones is a new *boarder* at this house.
Border—Boundary or frontier. The river forms a *border* between the two states.

45. **Boer**—Dutch colonist. He is a *Boer* from South Africa.
Boor—Ill-mannered person. He acted like a *boor.*

46. **Born**—Given birth to. Mamie was *born* in 1935.
Borne—Form of "to bear." The casket was *borne* to the grave.
Bourn (bourne)—Goal or limit. "The undiscovered country from whose *bourne* no traveler returns."

47. **Borough**—Governmental unit. She lives in the *borough* of Queens.
Borrow—To receive with the intention of returning. He wants to *borrow* my coat.
Burro—Donkey. I'll ride the horse; you ride the *burro.*

48. **Brake**—Device for stopping. The *brake* on this truck needs repair.
Break—To separate, destroy. Be careful not to *break* the glasses.

49. **Bread**—Food. Give her a slice of *bread*.
Bred—Hatched, born. This is a finely *bred* horse.

50. **Breadth**—Distance, width. The box is four inches in *breadth*.

Breath—Exhalation. His *breath* froze in the cold air.

Breathe—To inhale or exhale air. Please *breathe* slowly and deeply.

51. **Brewed**—Fermented, steeped. Jane *brewed* a cup of tea.

    Brood—Offspring. The hen had a large *brood* of chicks.

52. **Bridal**—Referring to a bride. You are invited to the *bridal* supper.

    Bridle—Headgear for an animal. The horse objects to his new *bridle*.

53. **Britain**—Short for *Great Britain*. London is the capital of *Britain*.

    Briton—An Englishman. He is proud to be a *Briton*.

54. **Broach**—To bring up (verb). Let's not *broach* that subject.

    Brooch—Pin with a clasp. She wore an expensive *brooch*.

55. **Build**—To make, establish. Let's *build* our home here.

    Billed—Past tense of "to bill." He was *billed* for the entire sum.

56. **Bullion**—Ingots. Much gold *bullion* is stored at Fort Knox.

    Bouillon—Broth. The patient ate a cup of chicken *bouillon*.

57. **Calendar**—Table, register. I have no appointments on my *calendar.*

    Calender—Machine with rollers. The *calender* gave the cloth a glossy finish.

    Colander—Pan with perforations. Use a *colander* for washing lettuce.

58. **Calvary**—Name of a hill outside Jerusalem. Jesus was crucified on *Calvary.*

    Cavalry—Troops on horseback. Stonewall Jackson was a *cavalry* leader.

59. **Cannon**—Large gun. Men pulled the *cannon* into position.

    Canon—Law or rule. He lives by the *canon* of good taste.

60. **Canvas**—Cloth. The *canvas* was stiff with mud.
    Canvass—To solicit, request. Please *canvass* the block for donations.
61. **Capital**—For all meanings other than "a building." He raised *capital* for the work.
    Capitol—A building. Many sightseers go to the state *capitol.*
62. **Carat**—Weight. The stone weighs two *carats.*
    Caret—Proofreading mark. Insert a *caret* to show the missing letter.
    Carrot—Vegetable. Scrape the *carrots* slowly.
63. **Casual**—Not planned, incidental. This is a *casual* visit.
    Causal—Relating to cause and effect. A *causal* factor in his decision was illness.
64. **Ceiling**—Overhanging expanse. Your room has a high *ceiling.*
    Sealing—Fastening, closing. Try *sealing* the envelope more carefully.
65. **Censer**—Incense burner. There is a lovely ornamented *censer* in the church.
    Censor—To examine. I do not wish you to *censor* my mail.
    Censure—To condemn. The judge will strongly *censure* your action.
66. **Cent**—Coin. It's not worth a *cent.*
    Scent—Odor. The *scent* of the skunk was powerful.
67. **Charted**—Mapped. The trapper *charted* the wilderness.
    Chartered—Hired, engaged. We *chartered* a bus for the picnic.
68. **Chased**—Pursued, followed. Joe often *chased* after pretty girls.
    Chaste—Pure, unsullied. A *chaste* reputation is considered priceless.
69. **Choir**—Group of singers. Joy sings in a church *choir* every week.

Quire—Measurement of paper. He used up a *quire* of paper.

70. **Choose**—To pick out, select. I do not *choose* to go to-day.

   Chose—Past tense of "to choose." I *chose* not to go yesterday.

71. **Chord**—Combination of musical tones. The pianist played the opening *chords*.

   Cord—String or rope. Tie this package with a strong *cord*.

72. **Cite**—To summon, quote. Please *cite* your authority.

   Sight—View, vision. The valley was a beautiful *sight*.

   Site—Location. This is a good *site* for our camp.

73. **Claws**—Talons, curved nails. This kitten has sharp *claws*.

   Clause—Group of words. This sentence has no dependent *clause*.

74. **Climactic**—Pertaining to climax. This was the *climactic* scene in the drama.

   Climatic—Pertaining to climate. He likes the *climatic* conditions in Florida.

75. **Clothes**—Body covering. Tom bought a suit of *clothes*.

   Cloths—Pieces of cloth. Dirty dish *cloths* hung near the sink.

76. **Coarse**—Unrefined, common. The driver's *coarse* speech offended the passengers.

   Course—Way or passage. He took the easy *course*.

77. **Coma**—Unconsciousness. Mr. Jones fell into a deep *coma*.

   Comma—Mark of punctuation. This word should be followed by a *comma*.

78. **Complacent**—Smug, self-satisfied. Your attitude is annoyingly *complacent*.

   Complaisant—Obliging. The patient was *complaisant* about hospital routine.

79. **Complement**—Something that completes. This necklace will *complement* your dress.

Compliment—Flattery. She enjoyed the *compliment* paid to her.

80. **Comprehensible**—Understandable. To be *comprehensible* use nontechnical language.
    Comprehensive—Inclusive, including much. This was a *comprehensive* account of the battle.

81. **Confidant**—One trusted with secrets. Jill made David her *confidant*.
    Confident—Assured, certain. Jack was *confident* of success.

82. **Conscience**—Sense of right and wrong. His *conscience* began to bother him.
    Conscious—Awake, able to feel and think. The injured boy was still *conscious*.

83. **Conscientiousness**—Uprightness, honesty. The notary was rewarded for his *conscientiousness*.
    Consciousness—Awareness. The victim died before regaining *consciousness*.

84. **Consul**—An official. He called the American *consul* at Naples.
    Council—Assembly, group. This is a *council* of older citizens.
    Counsel—Advice. The physician gave me sound *counsel*.

85. **Coral**—Skeletons of marine animals. The ship foundered on a *coral* reef.
    Corral—Pen or enclosure. This ranch needs a better *corral* for horses.

86. **Core**—Center. The *core* of an apple is not edible.
    Corps—Group of people. They were assigned to a *corps* of engineers.
    Corpse—Dead body. The *corpse* was carried to the local cemetery.

87. **Corporal**—Concerning the body (adjective), or low-ranking officer (noun). The teacher does not approve of *corporal* punishment. He was promoted to the rank of *corporal*.

Corporeal—Material, tangible. He left no *corporeal* property.

88. **Costume**—Clothing. Your *costume* is too colorful.
    Custom—Established practice. It was his *custom* to walk there every day.

89. **Creak**—To make a sound. He felt as though his very bones would *creak*.
    Creek—Small stream. Bill waded in the *creek*.

90. **Crews**—Seamen or groups of persons. The *crews* of all vessels were discharged.
    Cruise—Voyage. They left on a *cruise* around the world.

91. **Currant**—Small, seedless raisin. This recipe for fruit cake requires the use of *currants*.
    Current—A stream (noun) or contemporary (adjective). This river has a swift *current*. I like to read about *current* events.

92. **Cymbal**—Musical instrument. Is the *cymbal* made of brass or bronze?
    Symbol—Sign or token. The flag is a *symbol* of our country.

93. **Dairy**—Milk enterprise. He drove the cows from the field to the *dairy*.
    Diary—Daily record. Eleanor kept a *diary* during her entire trip.

94. **Days**—Plural of "day." I was in the hospital for ten *days*.
    Daze—To dazzle or stupefy. The policeman was *dazed* by a sharp blow.

95. **Dear**—Beloved, precious, expensive. Bill is my *dear* friend.
    Deer—Animal. Usually only the male *deer* has antlers.

96. **Decease**—Death. He was buried two days after his *decease*.
    Disease—Sickness. This *disease* must run its course.

97. **Decent**—Respectable, suitable. Please wear a *decent* hat.

Descent—Act of descending. The *descent* from the mountain top was slow.

Dissent—To differ, disagree. I *dissent* from your opinion.

98. **Definite**—Explicit, clear. The speaker made a *definite* proposal.

   Definitive—Decisive, final, complete. This is the *definitive* biography of Mrs. Siddons.

99. **Dependence**—Condition of being supported. My *dependence* upon you is complete.

   Dependents—Those supported by others. He claimed six *dependents* on his tax return.

100. **Deprecate**—To express disapproval. He *deprecated* his own efforts.

   Depreciate—To lower in value. The property *depreciated* quickly.

101. **Des′ ert**—Barren ground. The *desert* is two hundred miles wide.

   De sert′—To leave behind. Don't *desert* your friends.

   Dessert—Sweet food. Ice cream is my favorite *dessert*.

102. **Detract**—To lower the quality of, to reduce the value of. His loud voice *detracted* from his personality.

   Distract—To divert. Don't *distract* me with radio music.

103. **Device**—Contrivance (noun). The inventor came up with a clever *device*.

   Devise—To make, invent (verb). The coach will *devise* a plan for winning the game.

104. **Die**—To cease to live. Everyone must *die* sometime.

   Dye—To color. I wish to *dye* this dress.

105. **Dining**—Eating. This is a pretty *dining* room.

   Dinning—Pertaining to noise, uproar. The sound of the wheels was *dinning* in my ears.

106. **Discomfit**—To frustrate, thwart. Your proposal will *discomfit* my hopes and plans.

   Discomfort—Uneasiness, distress. His broken leg caused him *discomfort*.

107. **Discreet**—Judicious, thoughtful. You should be more *discreet* when talking to the boss.
Discrete—Separate, distinct. These two problems are *discrete*.

108. **Divers**—Several or sundry. She has *divers* means of support.
Diverse—Different, varied. Their personalities were powerful but *diverse*.

109. **Dual**—Twofold. The actress has a *dual* role in this play.
Duel—Combat. Hamilton and Burr fought a *duel*.

110. **Due**—Payable. The money is *due* today.
Do—To perform, act. Kindly *do* as your foreman suggests.

111. **Emigrate**—To leave a country. The foreman *emigrated* from Poland.
Immigrate—To enter a country. Many people have tried to *immigrate* to this country.

112. **Eminent**—Noteworthy, outstanding. Mr. Hughes is an *eminent* lawyer.
Imminent—Near at hand. Outbreak of war is *imminent*.

113. **Envel′ op**—To cover, wrap up. Fire caused smoke to *envelop* the block.
En′ velope—A covering. This *envelope* has no postage stamp.

114. **Errand**—Trip or task. Please run this *errand* for me.
Errant—Roving, wandering, mistaken. Please correct your *errant* behavior.
Arrant—Notorious. The soldier proved himself an *arrant* coward.

115. **Ever**—Always. He is *ever* in a jovial mood.
Every—Without exception. *Every* person present will please stand.

116. **Exalt**—To raise, praise. Shall we *exalt* God the Father?
Exult—To rejoice. Don't *exult* over your victory.

117. **Exceptionable**—Objectionable. Your constant tardiness is *exceptionable*.

     Exceptional—Out of the ordinary. Joy's singing is *exceptional*.

118. **Extant**—Still existing. He is the greatest musician *extant*.

     Extent—Size, length. What is the *extent* of your farm?

     Extinct—No longer existing. The dinosaur is an *extinct* beast.

119. **Factitious**—Artificial. The greatest *factitious* need of today is money.

     Fictitious—Imaginary. His account of the journey was entirely *fictitious*.

120. **Fain**—Ready, eager (rarely used). She would *fain* go with you.

     Feign—To invent, fabricate. The sailor *feigned* illness.

121. **Faint**—To lose consciousness. I feel as if I am about to *faint*.

     Feint—To pretend, deceive. The player *feinted* his opponent out of position.

122. **Fair**—All uses except those for "fare." The day was cold and *fair*.

     Fare—To travel (verb); transportation money (noun). I shall soon *fare* forth. Please pay your *fare*.

123. **Find**—To discover. Try to *find* happiness where you can.

     Fined—Punished. The motorist was *fined* fifty dollars.

124. **Fir**—Tree. This is a grove of beautiful *firs*.

     Fur—Animal hair. This coat has a collar of *fur*.

125. **Flair**—Talent, ability. She has a certain *flair* for designing clothes.

     Flare—To blaze up. The fire suddenly *flared* up.

126. **Flea**—Insect. The *flea* is a small, wingless creature.

     Flee—To run away. We had to *flee* from the burning house.

127. **Flour**—Ground grain. This is enough *flour* to feed us.

    Flower—A blossom. The rose is Gray's favorite *flower.*

128. **Flout**—To mock, to scoff. She was determined to *flout* all convention.

    Flaunt—To make a gaudy display. He *flaunted* his new prosperity all over the city.

129. **Fondling**—Caressing, coddling. Will you stop *fondling* that cat?

    Foundling—Abandoned child. This is a home for *foundlings.*

130. **Forbear**—To refrain. I cannot *forbear* telling you this.

    Forebear—Ancestor. His *forebears* came from Greece.

131. **Foreword**—Preface, introduction. This book needs no *foreword.*

    Forward—Movement onward. The troops marched *forward.*

132. **Formally**—Ceremoniously. The envoy greeted us *formally.*

    Formerly—Earlier. He was *formerly* a champion.

133. **Fort**—Enclosed place, fortified building. The attackers burned the *fort.*

    Forte—Special accomplishment. His *forte* is outdoor cooking.

134. **Forth**—Onward. I shall be with you from this day *forth.*

    Fourth—Next after third. The *Fourth* of July is a holiday.

135. **Freeze**—To congeal with cold. He asked me to *freeze* the vegetables.

    Frieze—Architectural term. The castle had several beautiful *friezes* on the walls.

136. **Funeral**—Ceremonies at burial. The *funeral* was attended by hundreds of friends.

    Funereal—Sad, dismal. Molly wore a *funereal* look.

137. **Gait**—Manner of moving. This saddle horse has four excellent *gaits*.
Gate—Door or opening. Open the *gate* and come in.

138. **Gamble**—To wager, bet. He *gambled* on cards and dice.
Gambol—To skip about. The children *gamboled* on the village green.

139. **Genius**—Great ability. Beethoven was a man of *genius*.
Genus—Class, kind. What is the *genus* of this plant?

140. **Gibe**—To scorn or sneer at. I'm trying hard; don't *gibe* at me.
Jibe—Same meaning as "gibe," but also "to change direction." The boat *jibed* twice on the homeward run.

141. **Gild**—To overlay with gold. Please *gild* this vase.
Guild—Association, union. Sam belonged to a *guild* of craftsmen.

142. **Gilt**—Gold on surface. This glass has a layer of *gilt*.
Guilt—Wrongdoing, crime. He immediately announced his *guilt*.

143. **Gorilla**—Manlike ape. This *gorilla* is five feet tall.
Guerrilla—Irregular soldier. He belonged to a band of *guerrillas*.

144. **Gourmand**—Large eater. Diamond Jim Brady was a *gourmand*.
Gourmet—Fastidious eater, epicure. Many French people are notable *gourmets*.

145. **Grip**—Act of holding firmly. He took a firm *grip* on the tire.
Gripe—To pinch, to distress. What he ate had *griped* his digestive system.

146. **Grisly**—Horrible, ghastly. The execution was a *grisly* scene.
Gristly—Pertaining to tough, elastic tissue. This is a *gristly* cut of meat.
Grizzly—Grizzled, gray; pertaining to the animal. There is only one *grizzly* bear in the zoo.

147. **Hail**—To greet. We *hailed* him as our leader.
     Hale—Healthy, vigorous. He wanted to be *hale* in mind and body.
148. **Hair**—Threadlike outgrowth. He had no *hair* on his head.
     Hare—Rabbit. The dog chased the *hare* for an hour.
149. **Hart**—Male deer. The old *hart* was king of the forest.
     Heart—Muscular organ. His *heart* was beating quickly.
150. **Heal**—To make sound, well. My hope is to *heal* you in mind and body.
     Heel—Part of the foot. His *heel* was punctured by a nail.
151. **Hear**—To become aware of sounds. I can't *hear* you.
     Here—In this place. Will you be *here* with me?
152. **Hoard**—Laid-up store. Here is where he had his *hoard* of money.
     Horde—Crowd. A *horde* of riders clattered toward us.
153. **Hole**—Cavity. The boys dug a *hole* in the ground.
     Whole—Intact, complete. I've told you the *whole* story.
154. **Holy**—Sacred, consecrated. A church is a *holy* place.
     Wholly—Completely, entirely. I'm *wholly* on your side.
155. **Hoping**—Wanting, desiring. I'm *hoping* you will accept my invitation.
     Hopping—Leaping, springing. I'm *hopping* a train tonight.
156. **Human**—A person. He was a real *human*, not a mere animal.
     Humane—Tender, merciful, considerate. He was a *humane* ruler of his people.
157. **Idle**—Worthless, useless, pointless. We engaged in *idle* talk.
     Idol—Image. Ben made an *idol* of prestige.
158. **Immunity**—Exemption from duty. Heart disease gave him *immunity* from military service.

Impunity—Exemption from punishment. He could eat with *impunity* whatever he pleased.

159. **Impassable**—Not passable. The road over the mountain was *impassable*.
     Impossible—Incapable of being accomplished. The order was *impossible* to carry out.

160. **Incidence**—Range of occurrence, influence. The *incidence* of influenza was high that winter.
     Incidents—Events, happenings. Which *incidents* of your trip did you enjoy the most?

161. **Indict**—To accuse, charge with crime. He was *indicted* for theft.
     Indite—To write, compose. He *indited* a beautiful letter to the sorrowing widow.

162. **Ingenious**—Clever, tricky. This is an *ingenious* computer.
     Ingenuous—Innocent, artless. She is an *ingenuous* young girl.

163. **Invade**—To enter, intrude. The soldiers were soon ordered to *invade* our country.
     Inveighed—Attacked in words, assailed. He *inveighed* against all his enemies.

164. **Its**—Possessive pronoun. This company should have *its* proper place in history.
     It's—"It is." *It's* a delightful day.

165. **Jealous**—Resentful, envious. Mary is *jealous* of Jane's beauty.
     Zealous—Diligent, devoted. The senator was *zealous* in committee work.

166. **Knave**—Unprincipled man or boy. The attorney called the gangster a *knave*.
     Nave—Part of a church. Chairs were placed in the *nave*.

167. **Knew**—To have fixed in mind or memory. The salesman *knew* all the buyer's objections.
     New—Of recent origin. This is a *new* model.

168. **Know**—To understand, perceive. Do you *know* how far it is to town?

No—Word used to express denial, dissent. *No*, I shall not go with you.

169. **Later**—Referring to time. It's *later* than you think.
Latter—Second of two. I prefer the *latter* course of action.

170. **Lead**—Conduct, guide. John will *lead* the choral group.
Lead—A metal. This is a *lead* pipe.
Led—Past tense of "to lead." Grant *led* his soldiers into Vicksburg.

171. **Leaf**—Outgrowth of a stem. This is a lovely oak *leaf.*
Lief—Gladly, willingly. I'd as *lief* go as stay.

172. **Lean**—Scant of fat, flesh. This is a *lean* strip of bacon.
Lien—Legal right. He procured a *lien* on the property.

173. **Least**—Smallest, slightest. This was the *least* of my worries.
Lest—For fear that. Please keep writing *lest* we forget you.

174. **Lessen**—To become less, diminish. Now all your financial problems will *lessen.*
Lesson—Something to be learned. May this be a *lesson* to you.

175. **Levee**—Embankment. The river overflowed the *levee.*
Levy—To impose. The judge will *levy* a large fine.

176. **Lie**—Falsehood. He told me a *lie.*
Lye—Alkaline substance. Keep this bottle of *lye* away from children.

177. **Lifelong**—For all one's life. His *lifelong* desire was to go to Europe.
Livelong—Whole, entire. Birds sing the *livelong* day.

178. **Lightening**—Making less heavy. His kindness was *lightening* my weight of sorrow.
Lightning—Discharge of electricity. The rain was preceded by thunder and *lightning.*

179. **Lineament**—Feature, characteristic. What is the most noticeable *lineament* of his face?
Liniment—Medicated liquid. The trainer rubbed the boxer's legs with *liniment*.

180. **Liqueur**—Highly flavored alcoholic drink. Joe's favorite after-dinner *liqueur* was chartreuse.
Liquor—Distilled or spirituous beverage. Scotch was Abe's favorite *liquor.*

181. **Loan**—Act of granting, lending. I secured a *loan* of fifty dollars.
Lone—Solitary, standing apart. He was the *lone* rebel in the office.

182. **Loose**—Not fastened tightly. A *loose* wire caused all the trouble.
Lose—To suffer the loss of. Don't *lose* what you have gained.
Loss—A defeat. He felt keenly the *loss* of the money.

183. **Mail**—Letters, etc. The *mail* came at ten o'clock.
Male—Masculine. This cat is *male*.

184. **Main**—Chief, principal. Is this the *main* highway?
Mane—Long hair. The horse's *mane* was filled with cockleburs.

185. **Manner**—Way of doing. They treated us in a civilized *manner.*
Manor—Landed estate. Sir Charles is lord of the *manor.*

186. **Mantel**—Shelf. The *mantel* above the fireplace is of sturdy oak.
Mantle—Loose covering. Has the *mantle* of Moses descended upon this judge?

187. **Marshal**—Officer. The *marshal* arrested him.
Martial—Warlike. The governor placed the community under *martial* law.

188. **Material**—Crude or raw matter, substance. What is the *material* in your dress?
Matériel—Equipment in general. This military campaign required vast *matériel.*

189. **Maybe**—Perhaps. *Maybe* she doesn't like you.
May be—Verb form expressing possibility. It *may be* going to rain this afternoon.

190. **Meat**—Flesh. His favorite foods are *meat* and potatoes.
Meet—To come into contact. We plan to *meet* tomorrow.

191. **Medal**—Commemorative design. The major gave him a *medal* for bravery.
Meddle—To interfere. Please don't *meddle* in my business.
Metal—A hard substance obtained from ores. Gold, silver, and copper are *metals*.
Mettle—Disposition, temper. The battle revealed the soldier's *mettle*.

192. **Miner**—One who extracts minerals. He is a *miner* from Pennsylvania.
Minor—Person under legal age. A *minor* has no voting privileges.

193. **Moat**—Trench. The *moat* around the castle was filled with water.
Mote—Particle, speck. He had a *mote* of dust in each eye.

194. **Moors**—Mohammedans. Many *Moors* live in North Africa.
Moors—Open land. These flowers came from the Scottish *moors*.
Mores—Folkways, customs. *Mores* here differ from those in my country.

195. **Moral**—Good or proper. His *moral* code was high.
Morale—Condition of the spirit, state of being. The *morale* of the workers was excellent.

196. **Morning**—Early part of the day. We shall leave early tomorrow *morning*.
Mourning—Sorrowing, grieving. The *mourning* family went to the cemetery.

197. **Motif**—Theme or subject. What is the *motif* of that composition?

Motive—Spur or incentive. The *motive* of the murder was revenge.

198. **Naval**—Pertaining to ships. England was a great *naval* power.
     Navel—Pit or depression on the abdomen. He suffered a wound near his *navel*.

199. **Of**—Preposition with many meanings. He is a native *of* Ohio.
     Off—Away from. The car rolled *off* the highway.

200. **On**—Preposition with many meanings. Please put the bread *on* the table.
     One—Single unit or thing. He bought *one* orange for five cents.

201. **Oracle**—Place or medium for consulting gods. The senator visited the Delphic *oracle*.
     Auricle—Anatomical term. The *auricle* of her left ear was infected.

202. **Oral**—Spoken. The message was *oral*, not written.
     Aural—Pertaining to the sense of hearing. After the accident, his *aural* sense was below normal.

203. **Ordinance**—Rule, decree. There is a city *ordinance* against double parking.
     Ordnance—Military weapons. Captain Baker is an instructor of *ordnance* at West Point.

204. **Oscillate**—To swing, vibrate. The pendulum of the clock *oscillates* smoothly.
     Osculate—To kiss. Some explorers say Eskimos do not *osculate*.

205. **Pail**—Bucket or other container. Please fetch a *pail* of water.
     Pale—Of whitish appearance. My face turned *pale* in fear.

206. **Pain**—Suffering, distress. John had a *pain* in his back.
     Pane—Plate of glass. The baseball shattered the *pane*.

207. **Pair**—Two of a kind. This is a new *pair* of gloves.
     Pare—To peel. He *pared* a basket of apples.

208. **Palate**—Roof of the mouth. Peanut butter sticks to my *palate*.
Palette—Board for painters. The artist mixed an array of autumn colors on his *palette*.
Pallet—Small, makeshift bed. I was stiff and sore from a night spent on that *pallet*.

209. **Passed**—Moved by. The car *passed* us at a high speed.
Past—Just gone by. The *past* year was a good one for me.

210. **Peace**—Freedom from disturbance. What this world needs is *peace*.
Piece—Portion. Please give me a *piece* of pie.

211. **Pedal**—Lever. One *pedal* of the organ needed repair.
Peddle—To hawk, sell at retail. He *peddled* fresh fruits in a residential section.

212. **Pendant**—An ornament. She wore a gold *pendant* around her neck.
Pendent—Hanging or suspended. The *pendent* tapestry was Oriental.

213. **Persecute**—To oppress, harass. The Pilgrims were *persecuted* because of their religious beliefs.
Prosecute—To bring legal proceedings. The district attorney *prosecuted* the case against me.

214. **Personal**—Private. This is your *personal* property.
Personnel—Body of persons. This company has recruited interesting *personnel*.

215. **Petition**—A request. The manager read our *petition* for a coffee break.
Partition—Division, separation. Only a thin *partition* separated the two rooms.

216. **Physic**—Medicine. The physician recommended a strong *physic*.
Physique—Body structure. He has a robust *physique*.
Psychic—Pertaining to the mind or soul. The gypsy claimed *psychic* powers.

217. **Pillar**—Upright shaft. The ceiling was supported by eight *pillars*.

Pillow—Support for the head. He sleeps without a *pillow.*

218. **Pistil**—Seed-bearing organ. This is the *pistil* of a flowering plant.
Pistol—Small firearm. The sheriff carried his *pistol* in a holster.

219. **Plain**—Simple, or a level stretch of ground. He prefers *plain* foods. This *plain* contains hundreds of acres.
Plane—Carpenters' tool, or level of existence. Try smoothing it with a *plane.* Your families are on the same financial *plane.*

220. **Portion**—Part, quantity. This is a larger *portion* of the roast.
Potion—A drink. He drank the fiery *potion.*

221. **Pray**—To beseech, entreat. Please *pray* for my safety.
Prey—Plunder, booty. The eagle is a bird of *prey.*

222. **Precede**—To come or go before. Will you *precede* me into the room?
Proceed—To advance. He then *proceeded* to the next town.

223. **Prescribe**—To direct, order. The physician will *prescribe* a cure.
Proscribe—To banish, to outlaw. Caesar ordered that he be *proscribed.*

224. **Principal**—Chief, foremost. He had a *principal* part in the action.
Principle—Rule or truth. This is a sound *principle* to follow.

225. **Prophecy**—Prediction (noun). What is your *prophecy* about the future?
Prophesy—To foretell (verb). He could *prophesy* the results.

226. **Propose**—To put forth a plan. I *propose* that we take a vote.
Purpose—Intention, aim. What is your *purpose*?

227. **Quarts**—Measure. This bucket will hold eight *quarts.*

Quartz—Mineral. The geologist discovered *quartz* deposits near here.

228. **Quay**—Wharf. The ship was anchored a hundred yards from the *quay*.

Key—Instrument for locking, unlocking. Sue lost the *key* to her apartment.

229. **Quiet**—Still, calm. It was a *quiet* meeting.

Quit—To stop, desist. He *quit* his job on Friday.

Quite—Positive, entirely. I have not *quite* finished the book.

230. **Rabbit**—A rodent of the hare family. Mrs. MacGregor prepared a *rabbit* stew.

Rabid—Extreme, intense, or affected with rabies. He was known as a *rabid* partisan.

Rarebit—Welsh rabbit. The pronunciation should be "Welsh rabbit," not "Welsh *rarebit*."

231. **Rain**—Precipitation. We had four inches of *rain* last week.

Reign—Rule. Queen Elizabeth I had a long *reign*.

Rein—Check, curb. Lena could not *rein* in her mare going for the barn.

232. **Raise**—To lift, elevate. Please *raise* your eyes and look at me.

Raze—To tear down. The wreckers will *raze* the building.

Rise—To get up. When the president enters, everyone should *rise*.

233. **Rebound**—To spring back. His spirits *rebounded* at the good news.

Redound—To have a result or effect. Your excellent performance will *redound* to your credit.

234. **Reck**—To have care or concern. He *recks* not the costs involved.

Wreck—Destruction, damage. Hard living made him a *wreck* of a man.

235. **Reek**—Vapor, fume. There is a *reek* of turpentine in this room.

Wreak—To give vent to. He *wreaked* his anger on the secretarial pool.

236. **Respectably**—Properly, decently. The widow lived quietly and *respectably.*
Respectfully—With esteem, honor. He closed the letter "*Respectfully* yours."
Respectively—In order. He referred to Tom, Dick, and Harry *respectively.*

237. **Retch**—To try to vomit. He *retched* several times and then lay still.
Wretch—Miserable person. The poor *wretch* had threadbare clothing.

238. **Reverend**—Title for clergymen. The *Reverend* Stanley Smith is our pastor.
Reverent—Characterized by respect, sacredness. The audience was in a *reverent* mood.

239. **Right**—Correct, or direction. What is the *right* way to town? Turn *right*, not left.
Rite—Ceremony. The *rite* of burial was indeed solemn.

240. **Sail**—Material to catch wind. The *sails* were fluttering in the breeze.
Sale—Special offering of goods. He bought a suit that was on *sale*.

241. **Satire**—Work that expresses ridicule or contempt. He wrote a *satire* on office parties.
Satyr—Woodland deity, a lecherous man. John is more wolf than *satyr.*

242. **Scarce**—Not plentiful. The berries were *scarce* this year.
Scare—To startle, frighten. He was *scared* by news of the epidemic.

243. **Serf**—A slave. The manager treats me as though I were his *serf.*
Surf—Waves. The boat capsized in the heavy *surf.*

244. **Serge**—Fabric. This *serge* suit cost fifty dollars.
Surge—To swell, to increase suddenly. His anger *surged* at the insult.

245. **Shear**—To cut, clip. It is time to *shear* the sheep.
Sheer—Very thin. Her stockings were black and very *sheer.*

246. **Shone**—Glowed. Her face *shone* with happiness.
Shown—Appeared, made known. The salesmen have *shown* themselves to be capable.

247. **Shudder**—To shake or tremble. Reading about an accident makes me *shudder.*
Shutter—Screen or cover. The owner painted the *shutters* green.

248. **Sleight**—Deftness. He performed several *sleight* of hand tricks.
Slight—Slender, light. Jill is a very *slight* girl.

249. **Sole**—Single, one and only. Bernard was the *sole* survivor of the wreck.
Soul—Spiritual entity. The minister prayed for the dying man's *soul.*

250. **Stair**—A step. Mount the *stairs* carefully.
Stare—To gaze, glare. He stood there and *stared* at me.

251. **Stake**—Post, pole. Joan of Arc was burned at the *stake.*
Steak—Slice of meat. We served a four-pound *steak.*

252. **Stationary**—Fixed in position. This statue is obviously *stationary.*
Stationery—Paper for writing. I ordered a new box of *stationery.*

253. **Statue**—Sculptured likeness. His *statue* is in the museum.
Stature—Height. He was six feet in *stature.*
Statute—Law. This *statute* forbids gambling within city limits.

254. **Steal**—To take without permission. It is a crime to *steal* another's property.
Steel—Metal. The sword was made of *steel.*

255. **Stile**—A step. Use the *stile;* don't vault the fence.
Style—Manner of expression. This is furniture in the modern *style.*

256. **Stimulant**—Anything that stimulates. This drug is a heart *stimulant*.
     Stimulus—Something that rouses. His family's needs provided him with a *stimulus* to work hard.

257. **Straight**—Uncurved. The road ran *straight* for five miles.
     Strait—Narrow passageway. We crossed the *Strait* of Magellan.

258. **Suit**—Clothing. This is an expensive new *suit*.
     Suite—Set of rooms, or furniture. They engaged a *suite* of rooms at the hotel.

259. **Tail**—Rear appendage. This is the *tail* of a donkey.
     Tale—Story. He told us a *tale* of his trip to the planetarium.

260. **Taught**—Trained, instructed. We were *taught* how to add and subtract.
     Taut—Tightly stretched, tense. She gave us a *taut* smile.

261. **Than**—Particle denoting comparison. I am taller *than* Alfred.
     Then—At that time. It was *then* that he left.

262. **Their**—Possessive pronoun. *Their* faces all look alike to me.
     There—In or at that place. He was *there* on time.
     They're—Shortened form of "they are." *They're* improving all the time.

263. **Therefor**—For this, for that. He selected a car and paid cash *therefor*.
     Therefore—Consequently, hence. I have no money and *therefore* can't go.

264. **Thorough**—Complete. His examination was *thorough*.
     Though—Notwithstanding, although. *Though* you may be right, I can't agree with you.
     Threw—Tossed or hurled. They *threw* more wood on the fire.
     Through—From one end or side to the other. Let's walk *through* this field.

265. **Timber**—Building material. He bought *timber* for a new doghouse.

    Timbre—Quality of sound. I like the *timbre* of his voice.

266. **To**—Preposition with many meanings. Let's walk *to* town.

    Too—More than enough, in addition. You have already said *too* much.

    Two—Number after "one." There are *two* sides to this problem.

267. **Tortuous**—Winding, crooked. The path up the mountain is *tortuous*.

    Torturous—Full of, or causing, torture or pain. The surgeon began a *torturous* examination of my spine.

268. **Treaties**—Agreements. That country does not honor its *treaties*.

    Treatise—Systematic discussion. The professor wrote a *treatise* on this subject.

269. **Troop**—An assembled company. The *troop* of Girl Scouts made camp.

    Troupe—Traveling actors. He joined a *troupe* of Shakespearian actors.

270. **Urban**—Characteristic of a city. Do you prefer *urban* to rural life?

    Urbane—Suave, smooth. His manner and speech were *urbane*.

271. **Vain**—Worthless, empty. He made a *vain* attempt to save money.

    Vane—Direction pointer. This is a new weather *vane*.

    Vein—Blood vessel. The knife severed a *vein*, not an artery.

272. **Venal**—Corruptible, mercenary. The *venal* judge was soon removed from office.

    Venial—Excusable, pardonable. That was a *venial* sin, not a mortal one.

273. **Vial**—Small vessel. This is a *vial* of perfume.

Vile—Repulsive, offensive. His language was *vile*.

Viol—Musical instrument. The *viol* was often played in the sixteenth century.

274. **Vice**—Evil practice. The reformers are opposed to *vice* in every form.

Vise—Device for holding. The carpenter has many uses for a *vise*.

275. **Waist**—Middle section of a body. His *waist* is thirty-four inches.

Waste—To squander, to employ uselessly. Save your energy; don't *waste* it.

276. **Waive**—To relinquish, give up. Don't *waive* your right to a jury trial.

Wave—Ridge or swell of water. The *wave* tossed the small craft up.

277. **Want**—To wish or desire. I *want* to stay at home.

Wont—Accustomed, used. He was *wont* to take a nap every afternoon.

Won't—Contraction of "will not." I *won't* do what you ask.

278. **Weak**—Not strong. Your excuse is *weak*.

Week—Period of seven days. This has been an active *week* for me.

279. **Weather**—State of atmosphere. We had good *weather* for the trip.

Whether—Conjunction implying alternatives. We didn't know *whether* to stay or go.

280. **Were**—Form of verb "to be." *Were* you there yesterday?

We're—Contraction of "we are." *We're* going with you.

Where—In or at what place. *Where* did you put it?

281. **While**—During the time that. I was working *while* you ate.

Wile—Trick, stratagem. She practiced her feminine *wiles* on my roommate.

282. **Whose**—Possessive case of "who." *Whose* pencil is that?

Who's—Contraction of "who is." *Who's* going out for coffee today?

283. **Wrench**—To twist, pull, jerk. He *wrenched* his knee when he fell.

Rinse—To wash. He *rinsed* the clothes several times.

284. **Wring**—To squeeze, press. *Wring* out your bathing suit.

Ring—Band of metal. He paid little money for the wedding *ring*.

285. **Wry**—Twisted, distorted. He made a *wry* face.

Rye—Cereal grass. This is *rye* flour.

286. **Yeller**—One who shrieks or screams. He is the *yeller* on this team.

Yellow—A color. You are wearing a beautiful *yellow* dress.

287. **Yolk**—Part of an egg. The recipe calls for six *yolks*.

Yoke—Frame or bar. The oxen were harnessed with *yokes*.

288. **Yore**—Time long past. Knights were bold in days of *yore*.

Your—Belonging to or done by you. Is this *your* idea?

You're—Contraction of "you are." *You're* going to make more money soon.

289. **Yowl**—Howl, wail. The dog's *yowl* woke him up.

Yawl—Sailboat. We sailed the *yawl* across the bay.

290. **Yule**—Christmas. This is a wonderful *yule* log.

You'll—Contraction of "you will" or "you shall." If *you'll* help me, I shall try.

And here are ten more look-alikes and sound-alikes to add to your collection:

anecdote	brunet
antidote	brunette
beside	cede
besides	seed
blond	chafe
blonde	chaff

clench	foul
clinch	fowl
farther	juncture
further	junction

4

PRONOUNCE WORDS

CAREFULLY AND CORRECTLY

Just compare heart, beard, and heard,
Dies and diet, lord and word,
Sword and sward, retain and Britain,
(Mind the latter, how it's written)
Made has not the sound of bade;
Say, said, pay, paid, laid, but plaid.
                            —G. N. Trenité
                    Drop Your Foreign Accent

These lines of doggerel amusingly demonstrate that pronunciation is not a safe guide to spelling. A system which tolerates, for example, *cough* and *through* is quite imperfect. (A frequently cited illustration is that if you use the sound of *f* as the *gh* in *enough*, of *i* as the *o* in *women*, and of *sh* as the *ti* of *fiction*, you can spell *fish* as *ghoti*.) For another example of confusion confounded, consider the sound of *ain*, the sound we have in *pain*. It can be, and is, represented by these entirely different spellings: compl*ain*, p*ane*, r*eign*, v*ein*, camp*aign*, champ*agne*. In fact, pronunciation is so unreliable a guide to spelling that you can quite logically spell *coffee* as *kauphy*, with not a single corresponding letter in the two words.

Every modern American dictionary presents its own system of recording pronunciation. Your first move should be to find out about that system. Read the essay on pronunciation included in the front matter (first pages) of your dictionary; every reliable dictionary contains such an article. Study the full pronunciation

53

key provided on the inside of the front or back cover of your book, or in both places. Examine the pronunciation key appearing at the bottom of each page, or every other page, of your dictionary. Only after you have taken these steps are you in a position really to use your dictionary as a guide to pronunciation.

Pronunciation, as you already know and as your dictionary will again tell you, depends upon the *sound* given to alphabetical letters or letter combinations and upon the *accent* of emphasized syllables.

Dictionary Sound Systems

Dictionary-makers have had to make up systems for representing sounds because only twenty-six letters exist to represent some 250 common spellings of sounds. The best-known set of symbols for the sounds of language is the International Phonetic Alphabet (IPA). This alphabet, applicable to many languages, including English, is accurate, but the ordinary speaker will find it hard to follow.

Your most sensible approach is to study the "pronunciation word" that appears in parentheses immediately after an entry word. It is a respelling of the word, giving the sounds of vowels and consonants by syllables, according to the pronunciation key that your dictionary has adopted. (Every dictionary compiler has chosen anywhere from forty to sixty symbols that he thinks adequate to explain problems in pronunciation.) Study the key in your dictionary to find out the various sounds of letters and letter combinations as indicated in sample words.

As an indication of the kinds of information provided about pronunciation in your dictionary, see how it represents the varied sounds of, say, the letter *o*. You will find that the sounds of *o* are indicated by some or all of these symbols:

    o—as in *odd, hot, lot, ox*
    ō—as in *go, open, over, no*
    ô—as in *order, horn, ought*
    o͝o—as in *took, book, look*
    o͞o—as in *pool, ooze, boot, too*

Each of the signs (symbols appearing with words in a pronunciation key) is a kind of diacritical mark. (The word *diacritical*
comes from a Greek term meaning "capable of distinguishing,"
"distinctive.") Still other signs, or points, are occasionally added
to letters to indicate a particular sound value. Among these are
the *circumflex* (raison d'être), the *tilde* (cañon), the *umlaut*
(schön), and the *cedilla* (façade). Some dictionaries supply these
and other diacritical marks with individual words; other dictionaries provide a separate "foreign sounds" key. All diacritical
marks are inexact in suggesting the reproduction of sounds, but
their use is one further example of the pains dictionary makers
have taken in trying to provide a faithful record of the sounds of
language.

The matter of stress, or accent, is less involved than the pronunciation of sounds. But it is important. Examine the method
your dictionary employs for indicating where accents fall in given
entries. Some dictionaries provide both accent marks and syllabication periods (dots) in the entry word. Others use only dots
to indicate syllabication in the entry word and insert accent
marks in the "pronunciation word." Learn the methods your
dictionary has provided for indicating heavy (primary) stress and
less heavy (secondary) stress. Whatever devices your dictionary
uses are made fully clear in an article at the front of the book.

Although standard pronunciation will not always enable you to
spell correctly, the relationship between sound and spelling is
only occasionally illogical.

First, not all sounds and spellings differ so much as those just
cited. The examples given are designedly extreme. Actually,
some relationship often exists between sound and spelling; a large
number of words are spelled exactly as they sound, and many
others have sounds and spellings almost alike. The words *bat*,
red, and *top* are spelled as they sound to most people. Many
longer words are also spelled as they sound, especially if you
break them into syllables: *lone-li-ness, mem-o-ry, part-ner,* for
example. The situation is not without hope.

Second, many of the words which differ most greatly in sound
and spelling are those which you rarely need to use. Like almost
everyone else, including good spellers, you would look up such

words in a dictionary before attempting to write them; they do not have to be learned. Few people can spell, on demand, such a word as *phthisic*. They consult a dictionary, and so should you.

Third, actually *mispronouncing* words causes more trouble than does a difference between the spelling and sound of a correctly pronounced word. In other words, correct pronunciation is sometimes of little help in spelling, but *mispronouncing* often adds an additional hazard. You have noticed that this fact applies to some words in the list of "Look-Alikes and Sound-Alikes" beginning on page 22. It is probably improper pronunciation which would make you spell *Calvary* when you mean *cavalry*. *Affect* and *effect* look somewhat alike, but they do have different pronunciations as well as different meanings. A *dairy* is one thing; a *diary* is another and will be so indicated by correct pronunciation. There is some reason why, from sound, you might spell *crowd* as "croud" or *benign* as "benine." But there is no reason except poor pronunciation for spelling *shudder* as "shutter," *propose* as "porpose," or *marrying* as "marring."

Spelling consciousness, an *awareness* of words, depends in part on correct pronunciation. Properly pronouncing the following words will help some people to spell them correctly. Mispronouncing them will cause nearly everyone spelling trouble. Look at each word, as suggested on page 20, until you are fully aware of it. Pronounce each word correctly, consulting your dictionary often and carefully.

The list is merely suggestive; people mispronounce so many words in so many different ways that no list can be complete. But the author has encountered faulty spellings of the words listed here and suspects that they represent fairly general mispronunciations. For other examples, consult the list beginning on page 22. The first part of the following list deals with perfectly good words that have been confused. The second part reveals pronunciations resulting in nonexistent, incorrect words.

Words Confused in Pronunciation

1. caliber
   caliper
2. carton
   cartoon
3. casualty
   causality
4. celery
   salary
5. cemetery
   symmetry
6. color
   collar
7. concur
   conquer
8. dinghy
   dingy
9. elicit
   illicit

10. errand
    errant
11. faucet
    forceps
12. finally
    finely
13. gesture
    jester
14. gig
    jig
15. impostor
    imposture
16. minister
    minster
17. pastor
    pasture
18. plantiff
    plaintive

19. relic
    relict
20. sculptor
    sculpture
21. sense
    since
22. specie
    species
23. tenet
    tenant
24. veracity
    voracity
25. way
    whey

CORRECT	INCORRECT
corsage (small bouquet)	*corsarge* or *cosarge*
exercise (physical activity)	*excercise*
garage (storage place)	*gararge*
height (distance from bottom to top)	*heighth*
imagine (to form an idea)	*imangine*
irrelevant (unrelated)	*irrevelant*
poem (literary composition)	*pome*
radio (transmission of sound waves)	*raido* or *radeo*
research (systematic inquiry)	*reaserch*
strategic (favorable or advantageous)	*stragetic*
temperature (degree of heat)	*tempreture*
third (Number 3 in a series)	*thrid* or *therd*
tragedy (serious drama or event)	*tradegy*

Incorrect Prefixes

You don't transpose or otherwise confuse letters as is done in the list above? Good. The misspellings do look senseless and are characteristic of poor spellers. But you may have difficulty pronouncing and spelling certain words which have prefixes. (A prefix is usually one syllable added to the beginning of a word to alter its meaning or create a new word. The syllable *pre* is itself a prefix meaning "before in time," "earlier than.") Many prefixes were borrowed from Latin and Greek and do cause some people trouble with pronunciation, and hence spelling. Here are a few examples of words beginning with *per, pre,* and *pro,* the only prefixes which cause real trouble in pronouncing and spelling English words:

CORRECT	INCORRECT
perform (to act, to do)	*preform*
perhaps (possibly, probably)	*prehaps*
perjury (breaking an oath)	*prejury*
perspiration (sweating)	*prespiration*
perversely (persisting in error)	*preversely*
precipitate (to cause action)	*percipitate*
professor (a teacher)	*perfessor* or *prefessor*
proposal (a plan, scheme)	*porposal* or *preprosal*

Added Vowels

Some words are misspelled because in pronouncing them an extra vowel is added. A list of them would not be long, but since many of them are frequently used they merit careful study. Mispronouncing them may cause you not only to misspell but also to be looked on as careless in speech or uneducated, or both.

CORRECT	INCORRECT
athletics (sports, games)	*athaletics* or *atheletics*
disastrous (causing harm, grief)	*disasterous*
entrance (act or point of coming in)	*enterance*
explanation (interpretation)	*explaination*

grievous (serious, grave)	*grievious*
Henry (proper name)	*Henery*
hindrance (obstacle, impediment)	*hinderance*
hundred (the number)	*hundered*
laundry (washing of clothes)	*laundery* or *laundary*
mischievous (prankish)	*mischievious*
monstrous (huge, enormous)	*monsterous*
nervous (emotionally tense)	*nerveous*
partner (associate)	*partener*
remembrance (souvenir, keepsake)	*rememberance*
similar (alike)	*similiar*
Spanish (pertaining to Spain)	*Spainish*
umbrella (shade or screen)	*umberella*

Dropped Vowels

There are many different ways to misspell words: you can do so by dropping vowels as well as by adding them. Educated speakers often drop vowels in pronouncing some words in the following list; therefore you should study this list carefully since even acceptable pronunciation is not always a sure guide. However, a few of these words could not be pronounced correctly from the faulty spelling shown—whole syllables would drop out. Only in highly informal speech or television advertising would *caramel* be pronounced *carmel*.

1. John's truck accidentally (not *accidently*) hit the child.
2. This is an *auxiliary* (not *auxilary*) gasoline tank.
3. The physician prescribed *beneficial* (not *benefical*) drugs.
4. The pianist gave a *brilliant* (not *brillant*) recital.
5. He is a soldier, not a *civilian* (not *civilan*).
6. This harsh *criticism* (not *critcism*) is merited.
7. She is a *conscientious* (not *conscientous*) housewife.
8. This *convenient* (not *convenent*) room is for your use.
9. John is *deficient* (not *deficent*) in his accounts.
10. Mary is an *efficient* (not *efficent*) typist.
11. Your face is *familiar* (not *familar*).

12. I seek your *financial* (not *financal*) help.
13. King Cole was a merry, *genial* (not *genal*) soul.
14. Beethoven was a man of *genius* (not *genus*).
15. Your sentence is *grammatically* (not *grammaticly*) sound.
16. The money is only *incidentally* (not *incidently*) important.
17. The chemistry *laboratory* (not *labratory*) is large.
18. I like to read good *literature* (not *literture*).
19. *Mathematics* (not *mathmatics*) deals with numbers.
20. A child is a *miniature* (not *minature*) man.
21. Your *opinion* (not *opinon*) is valid.
22. This is an *original* (not *orignal*) idea.
23. Sir Henry is a member of *Parliament* (not *Parliment*).
24. He is *proficient* (not *proficent*) as a manager.
25. Sue has an even *temperament* (not *temperment*).

In addition to these twenty-five words illustrated in sentences, check your pronunciation of the following. Some people slur over the vowels which are shown in bold face; some omit them entirely; some pronounce them with considerable stress. Pronounce each word as you normally do. If the letters in bold face are silent, or lightly stressed in your speech, you are likely to omit them from your spelling.

accompan**i**ment	d**i**fferent	mis**e**ry
acc**u**racy	fam**i**ly	Niag**a**ra
asp**i**rin	friv**o**lous	op**e**rate
bach**e**lor	hist**o**ry	partic**u**lar
bound**a**ry	ign**o**rant	priv**i**lege
cas**u**alties	length**e**ning	reg**u**lar
consid**e**rable	li**a**ble	scen**e**ry
crim**i**nal	lux**u**ry	sim**i**lar
def**i**nite	mag**a**zine	temper**a**ture
deliv**e**ry	mem**o**ry	vict**o**ry

Dropped Consonants

As we have noticed, spelling is definite, fixed, and unyielding. But not so with pronunciation, since that is constantly changing, differs from place to place, and is even varied on different occasions by the same speaker. The word *garden* is always spelled g-a-r-d-e-n, but it can be, and is, pronounced in half a dozen different ways. You can drop the *r* or retain it. You can use any of three different sounds for the two vowels in the word, with or without shadings of sound. Each of these pronunciations is correct and normally is completely understood when used.

Such variation in pronouncing words sometimes does cause spelling problems. If our visual memory of words is stronger than our auditory image, no harm is done. But when a letter is incorrectly omitted in pronouncing a word, we have to be on guard. The following representative list of words should be studied carefully. If you master this list, you will then be alert to still other words in which consonants are slurred over or remain silent. In each word the "offending" consonant is set in bold face; try to pronounce it fully, sounding it out as an aid to your auditory memory.

1. Mr. Avery is an old a**c**quaintance of mine.
2. The Ar**c**tic Circle is entirely imaginary.
3. This puts me in an awk**w**ard position.
4. He is a candi**d**ate for the office.
5. The driver was convicted of drunken**n**ess.
6. He stopped school in the ei**gh**th grade.
7. Mac grew up in a poor enviro**n**ment.
8. Feb**r**uary is the shortest month in the year.
9. He is opposed to all forms of govern**m**ent.
10. Karen is now a proud kin**d**ergarten pupil.
11. He owns a luc**r**ative business.
12. There are thousands of books in her lib**r**ary.
13. The barn was struck by light**n**ing.
14. You are per**h**aps too hasty in judging me.
15. Sam is proba**b**ly the best salesman in the company.
16. He purchased a large quan**t**ity of food.

17. This is a quarter, not a dime.
18. Mae did not seem to recognize me.
19. He was a good representative for the firm.
20. This statement surprised me.

In addition to these twenty illustrated words, and as a start on your additional list, pronounce each of the following as you ordinarily do. Perhaps your pronunciation will offer a clue to the cause of some of your misspellings. In each word, the "offending" consonant appears in bold face. Some of these consonants are silent or are slurred over.

accept	grandfather	recognize
acquire	handful	rheumatism
and	handle	rhythm
authentic	hustle	slept
column	identical	soften
condemn	kept	swept
consumption	landlord	tempt
contempt	listen	tentative
empty	nestle	trestle
except	often	used to
fascinate	prompt	wrestle
fasten	pumpkin	yellow

Unstressed Vowels

No words in English are more often misspelled than those which contain unstressed (or lightly stressed) vowels. An unstressed vowel, like the *a* in *dollar*, is uttered with little force; its sound is faint, indistinct, blurred.

A technical name, *schwa* (ə), is used to indicate this sound of unstressed vowels. It resembles a kind of "uh," a quiet sound much less vigorous than the stronger "uh" sound found in such words as *mud* and *rush*.

This unstressed vowel sound may be represented in spelling by any one of the letters: *a, e, i, o, u*.

a: grammar, sofa, above   o: professor, sponsor, occur

e: corner, model, establish   u: murmur, sulfur, luxury

i: nadir, peril, origin

The letter *y* is sometimes a vowel also. Its unstressed sound is illustrated in the word *martyr.*

Although the schwa sound ("uh") is the most frequent unstressed vowel sound, it is not the only one. An unstressed *i* sound appears in such words as *solid,* but is not always spelled as *i.* Note, for example, such words as priv*a*te, privil*e*ge. Still other unstressed vowel sounds occur in American speech, but isolating them is not helpful in learning to spell.

Unless both your auditory and visual memory are excellent, you must be suspicious of words containing lightly stressed syllables. It may help to exaggerate the "trouble spots" when you pronounce such words. Doing so may result in strained or even incorrect pronunciation, but you will increase your auditory image of words which, by sound alone, could be spelled in various ways. If the word *separate,* for example, causes you trouble, pronounce it "sep-A-rate" until you have its spelling firmly fixed in your visual, auditory, and motor images. Here is a representative list of sixty words often misspelled because of the unstressed vowels they contain:

academy	describe	hunger
accident	despair	hypocrisy
actor	develop	loafer
applicant	dilute	luxury
arithmetic	discipline	maintenance
benefit	distress	martyr
business	dollar	mathematics
calendar	ecstasy	medicine
category	excellent	model
clamor	existence	monastery
comparative	fakir	murmur
competitive	grammar	nadir
corner	hangar	occur
democracy	humorous	optimism

origin	professor	sofa
peril	propaganda	solid
politics	repetition	sponsor
possible	respectable	swindler
private	ridiculous	terror
privilege	separate	vulgar

Silent Letters

Some spelling authorities believe that the single greatest cause of misspelling connected with pronunciation is the silent letter. Sounds have been dropping out of our language for many centuries, but their disappearance has affected pronunciation much more than spelling. Actually, many letters no longer pronounced in certain words persist in our spelling, for no good reason: the *l* in such words as *could, would,* and *should* has been silent for hundreds of years, but it hangs on in spelling.

The problem is compounded when we realize that the majority of the letters in our alphabet appear as silent letters in one word or another:

de*a*d	*h*onest	ras*p*berry
dou*b*t	wei*r*d	of*t*en
s*c*ene	*k*nife	g*u*ess
han*d*some	sa*l*mon	ans*w*er
com*e*	*m*nemonics	ya*ch*t
of*f*	colum*n*	bou*gh*
si*g*n	fam*ou*s	

Some silent letters cause little difficulty in spelling. If you are "visual minded," you will automatically put a *k* in *knee* or a *g* in *gnat.* But other letters which are silent, or are so lightly sounded as to be almost unheard, do cause trouble. Here is a list of some common words which, in the pronunciation of most educated people, contain silent letters:

| align | bomb | condemn |
| benign | comb | crumb |

daughter	knave	psalm
dough	knee	psychology
dumb	kneel	through
eight	knit	thumb
fourth	knob	tomb
ghastly	knock	womb
ghost	knot	wrap
gnash	know	wreck
gnat	knuckle	wrench
gnaw	plumber	wretch
hymn	pneumatic	wring
indebted	pneumonia	write
knack	prompt	wrong

Once again, pronunciation is not a safe guide to spelling. But *faulty* pronunciation sometimes adds hazards. Pronouncing words correctly is at least a slight aid in correct spelling. Try to form clear and definite *auditory* and *visual* images of words whose pronunciation can compound spelling problems.

Here is a final list of words the careless pronunciation of which may cause misspellings. A few words in this list have been covered earlier in this chapter, but repetition may be useful.

accep (for *accept*)

accidently (for *accidentally*)

acrost (for *across*)

asprin (for *aspirin*)

atakt (for *attack*)

athaletics (for *athletics*)

attackted (for *attacked*)

bronokol (for *bronchial*)

carmel (for *caramel*)

cartoon (for *carton*)

colyum (for *column*)

congradulate (for *congratulate*)

defnite (for *definite*)

dintcha (for *didn't you*)

disasterous (for *disastrous*)

distrik (for *district*)

doncha (for *don't you*)

drownded (for *drowned*)

enviarment (for *environment*)

excep (for *except*)

famly (for *family*)

feller (for *fellow*)

figer (for *figure*)

finely (for *finally*)

gennelman (for *gentleman*)

gonna (for *going to*)

grievious (for *grievous*)

havncha (for *haven't you*)

hinderance (for *hindrance*)

histry (for *history*)

hundered (for *hundred*)

hyt-th (for *height*)

idenical (for *identical*)

incidently (for *incidentally*)

innerference (for *interference*)

inny (for *any*)

izda (for *is the*)

jester (for *gesture*)

jool (for *jewel*)

kep (for *kept*)

kintergarden (for *kindergarten*)

krool (for *cruel*)

laundery (for *laundry*)

literture (for *literature*)

manufacher (for *manufacture*)

mischievious (for *mischievous*)

modren (for *modern*)

monsterous (for *monstrous*)

nukular (for *nuclear*)

porpose (for *propose*)

practicly (for *practically*)

preform (for *perform*)

pressdent (for *president*)

probly (for *probably*)

progidy (for *prodigy*)

rasel (for *wrestle*)

reaserch (for *research*)

reconize (for *recognize*)

remembance (for *re-membrance*)

represenative (for *representa-tive*)

shudder (for *shutter*)

similiar (for *similar*)

slep (for *slept*)

smothertam (for *some other time*)

strenth (for *strength*)

suprise (for *surprise*)

tempature (for *temperature*)

tempermental (for *tempera-mental*)

tenative (for *tentative*)

tradegy (for *tragedy*)

tremenjous (for *tremendous*)

umberella (for *umbrella*)

use to (for *used to*)

vallable (for *valuable*)

victry (for *victory*)

walkin (for *walking*)

wanna (for *want to*)

whachusay (for *what did you say*)

whosit (for *who's it*)

willya (for *will you*)

woncha (for *won't you*)

wozzat (for *what's that*)

wunnerful (for *wonderful*)

wunst (for *once*)

youman (for *human*)

5

USE A DICTIONARY:

ETYMOLOGY

When you are suspicious of the spelling of any word you should check it immediately in your dictionary. "Doubt + dictionary = good spelling" is a reliable formula. However, it is a counsel of perfection, one that few of us are likely always to follow. Not only that, our sense of doubt may be so great that we spend half our writing time flipping dictionary pages rather than communicating and thus grow bored and frustrated.

Also, you may have tried to look up a word in the dictionary and been unable to find it. If your visual image of a word is weak, you can frustrate yourself even more: look for *agast* and you may give up before discovering that the word is *aghast*. You won't find *pharmacy* and *photograph* among words beginning with *f*. In fact, the confusion of sound and spelling has caused more than one reputable publishing firm seriously to consider preparing a dictionary for poor spellers. Such a dictionary would have been helpful to the man who was away on a trip and telephoned his secretary to send his gun to him at a hunting resort. The secretary could barely hear him (the connection was poor) and asked her boss to spell out what he wanted. "Gun," he shouted. "*G* as in *Jerusalem*, *u* as in *Europe*, *n* as in *pneumonia*." Whether or not he received his *jep* is unknown; maybe she sent him a dictionary instead.

The Dictionary as an Aid in Spelling

Even top-notch spellers consult a dictionary for the spelling of some words. You may not hesitate over *chiaroscuro* or *chimerical*, but you may need to look up *aficionado* or *solipsism* or *Yggdrasil*. Granting that few of us would use these words in the first place, most of us would check our doubts by consulting a dictionary each time. In addition, compound words frequently require hyphens for correct spelling; even superb spellers must look up many such words.

If you haven't done so yet, now would be a good time to get thoroughly acquainted with your dictionary. Better still, make it your friend; best of all, make it your constant companion. To paraphrase the words of Dr. Samuel Johnson, a great dictionary-maker, you would be well advised to give your days and nights to wise study of your dictionary.

Choice of a Dictionary

But you should know that there are dictionaries and dictionaries. Some, such as a pocket dictionary, are so small as to be virtually worthless save as a limited guide to spelling and pronunciation. Others, of fair size, may have been so hastily and carelessly produced that they are unreliable. Even the name "Webster" is no longer a guarantee of quality because as a label "Webster" is no longer copyrighted and appears alike in the titles of both reliable and unreliable dictionaries. You should have—and if you don't have, you should buy—a dictionary you can trust.

Suitable dictionaries are what economists refer to as "durable goods." It is well worth paying a few dollars to buy a good, hardbound dictionary that you can keep and use for many years. Equip yourself with a sufficiently large dictionary (approximately 100,000 entries), published by a reliable firm. These, for example, are good dictionaries:

The American Heritage Dictionary of the English Language
The Random House Dictionary of the English Language
Webster's New Collegiate Dictionary
Webster's New World Dictionary of the American Language

Word Derivation and Spelling

Etymology, a word taken from Greek, means an account of the history of a given word. More particularly, etymology deals with the origin and derivation of words. Knowing what a word comes from will often help you to spell it correctly. For example, the word *preparation* is derived from the Latin prefix *prae* ("beforehand") plus *parare* (meaning "to make ready"). Knowing this, and accenting the first *a* in *parare*, may help you to spell the word correctly: preparation, not preperation.

Similarly, our word *dormitory* (a building containing sleeping rooms) is derived from the Latin word *dormitorium*. Noting the first *i* in this Latin word, and perhaps also knowing that the French word for sleep is *dormir*, may help you to spell *dormitory* with an *i* and not an *a*.

A study of etymology primarily will aid one in building a vocabulary. But it also has its uses in learning to spell. Here are simplified comments on a few other common words which may fix this principle in your mind and lead to further study:

1. *Atmosphere.* This word meaning "the air," "the gaseous envelope surrounding the earth," is made from a learned borrowing from Greek, *atmo*, meaning "air," and *sphere*, meaning "a rounded body." Thus, *atmosphere* literally means "the earth's air."
2. *Biography.* The written account of another person's life is composed of *bio*, a prefix meaning "life," and *graphy*, a combining form denoting some process or form of writing, drawing, or representing.
3. *Calendar.* This word is descended from the Latin word for "account book," *calendarium*. Note the *a;* we frequently misspell the word as *calender* (a perfectly good word with an entirely different meaning).
4. *Consensus.* This word comes from the same Latin root as *consent* (*con* + *sentire*, to feel). Note the *s* in *sentire* and you will not spell the word *concensus*, as is frequently done.

5. *Denim.* This heavy twill cotton material takes its name from *Nimes*, a city in France.

6. *Equivalent.* This frequently misspelled word may be easier for you if you remember that it means "equal in value" and is derived from the prefix *equi* + *valere.* Accent the *val* sound in *valere* (value).

7. *Extravagance.* This word is composed of *extra* (beyond) plus the Latin word *vagans* (*vagari*, to wander). "Extravagance" is wandering beyond limits. Accent the letters *v-a-g* in the root word to insure correct spelling.

8. *Familiar.* This common word, often misspelled with an *e* where the second *a* should appear, is related to the Latin word *familia* (servants in a household).

9. *Finis.* This synonym for "end" has the same origin as the words *definite* and *finite.* Accent the *i* sound and come up with two *i*'s in this word.

10. *Medicine.* Many people tend to spell the second syllable of this word with an *e.* Its origin goes back to Latin *medicina* (*medicus*). Accent the *i* as an aid to correct spelling.

11. *Optimism.* This word comes to us by way of the French word *optimisme* (from Latin *optimus*, meaning "best"). Focus on the two *i*'s in *optimism.*

12. *Privilege.* From *privus* (private) plus *lex, legis* (law), this word can be remembered as "privy" (private) with the *y* changing to *i* plus *legal*, which fixes *leg* in *privilege.*

13. *Prologue.* Meaning a preliminary discourse or preface, this word is formed from a prefix meaning "before" and *logue*, a combining form denoting a spoken or written statement.

14. *Recommend.* This word comes from Latin *recommendare.* Think of it as *re* + *commend* and avoid that too-often-present double *c.*

15. *Sandwich.* This word owes its existence to the Earl of Sandwich (1718–1792), who was so fond of the gaming table that he refused to stop gambling for regular meals and instead ate bread with fillings of meat or fish. Remember that Sandwich was a gambler, not a

witch, and thus avoid the misspelling *sandwitch*. (Or maybe you would like to be able to eat a sandwich in the tropical Sandwich Islands, the former name for the Hawaiian Islands?)

16. *Sentiment*. This word derives from Latin *sentire*, meaning "to feel," "to perceive." Note the *i* in *sentire* and thus spell the word *sentiment*.

17. *Sophomore*. This word comes from the Greek word *sophos*, meaning "wise," and *moros*, meaning "foolish." There seem to be enough *o*'s in the original words to help us remember that we spell this word for "wise fool" as s*o*phom*o*re.

18. *Television*. *Tele* is a learned borrowing from Greek, meaning "distant." *Vision* means "sight." *Television* therefore means "distant sight," "seeing from afar."

19. *Thermostat*. This word comes from a Greek word, *thermos*, meaning "hot," plus another Greek word meaning "stationary." Remember the *o* in *thermos* and spell the word "therm*o*stat."

20. *Unanimous*. This word comes from Latin *unus*, meaning "one," plus *animus*, meaning "mind." Our word begins with the first syllable of *unus* and the first two syllables of *animus:* unani-. Now you will just have to remember to insert an *o* to come up with *unanimous*.

As a beginning for your list of words, the origin of which may help you with spelling, consult a good dictionary for the derivations of the following:

1. addict	8. dictaphone	15. monotone
2. amorphous	9. epilogue	16. pantomime
3. assess	10. exhilarate	17. photograph
4. astronomy	11. genesis	18. professor
5. atheist	12. hypodermic	19. recognize
6. auditorium	13. interdict	20. resemblance
7. boycott	14. kindergarten	

A considerable number of the memory devices beginning on page 152 are based upon etymology. Study them now or, when you come to them, refer again to this chapter.

6

USE A DICTIONARY:

ROOTS

One of the quickest, most useful, and easiest ways to learn correct spelling is to study how words are put together. Once you recognize the elements—the building blocks—of which words are made, hundreds, even thousands, of unfamiliar words will begin to have meaning and will be easy to spell.

These building blocks are *roots*, *combining forms*, *prefixes*, and *suffixes*.

The first and most important building block for words is *roots*. A root is the part of a word that indicates its primary, essential meaning. This meaning never changes, no matter what other letters or word parts are added.

Consider the root *vit-*, also spelled *viv-*, meaning "to live" or "life." From this building block come such words as these:

1. *vital*—(*vit-* means "life"; the suffix *-al* means "pertaining to"). Thus *vital* means necessary to life, full of life, or pertaining to life.
2. *vitamin*—(*vit-* plus the suffix *-amin*). A *vitamin* is a substance in food either useful or necessary for normal life in human beings and animals.
3. *vivacious*—a word meaning lively, active, full of life.
4. *vivid*—a word meaning lifelike, lively.
5. *revive*—a word formed from *viv-* and the prefix *re-*, meaning to bring back to life, to live again.

Other words formed from *vit-* are *vivacity*, *vivisection*, *vivify*, *survival*, *vitality*, *revival*, *vitalize*, *viviparous*. Note how knowing the meaning of this one root, *vit-*, makes clear the meaning of useful words perhaps unknown before.

Scores of word roots exist in English and are listed and defined in all superior dictionaries. When you come across a word that you suspect may be built from a root, try to find the part of the word you think is a root and consult your dictionary. Developing the habit of doing this will tremendously increase your ability to spell in easy, fun-producing steps.

1. *anim-*

   This root comes from Latin, in which the word *animus* meant "that which blows (wind) or is breathed (air)." In English, *anim-* means "soul," "life," "spirit." Note its appearance in these words:

   a. *animate* means "to give life to," "to make alive." Her appearance *animated* the party. He was *animated* by a desire to win. As an adjective *animate* means "alive" or "lively." Her laughter was an *animate* expression of her pleasure. Words related to *animate* are *animated*, *animation*, and *inanimate* (meaning "lifeless").

   b. *animosity* means "a feeling of ill will or enmity." The word formerly meant "having a high or lively spirit," but is now used to mean "vigorous dislike." The old settler felt *animosity* toward the newcomers.

   c. *animal* means "any living thing or being." It includes, in addition to humans, any living object: a fish, a bird, or an insect. All men, women, and children are *animals*. What's your favorite *animal* in the zoo? Related words are *animality* (animal nature) and *animalistic* (like an animal). *Animalism* is defined as "preoccupation with physical or sensual appetites."

   d. *unanimous* means "of a mind," "agreed," "in complete accord." The word is built from the Latin prefix *un-* (meaning "one"), the root *anim-* ("spirit," "mind," "heart"), and the suffix *-ous* ("being," "having"). The vote for the motion was *unanimous*. A related word is *unanimity*.

e. *equanimity* means "composure," "stability," "calmness." It comes from *equ-* ("even," "equal") and *anim-*. The speaker listened with *equanimity* to catcalls and shouts from the audience.

2. *annu-*

The root *annu-* (also spelled "enni") means "year."

a. *annual* means "yearly," "occurring or returning once a year." It is from the root *annu-* plus the Latin suffix *-al*. In botany, *annual* means "lasting only one year." The word also means "a pamphlet, periodical, or book published once a year." This company allows an *annual* vacation of three weeks. Corn is an *annual* crop.

b. *annuity* means "a specified income payable at stated intervals," the intervals usually being one year. Her *annuity* will last for a lifetime.

c. *biennial* means "happening, lasting, or enduring for two years." It is made up from the prefix *bi-* ("two") and *enni*: This is a *biennial* convention, taking place in even-numbered years.

d. *annals* means "a yearly record of events," although its meaning has been extended to cover greater periods of time, and frequently the word is applied to historical and other records: the *annals* of war, the *annals* of American history.

e. *centennial* comes from the Latin root *cent-* (meaning "one hundred") and *enni-*. The word means "lasting one hundred years," "a hundredth celebration or anniversary," "happening once every hundred years." The *centennial* of the founding of this town was celebrated a year ago.

3. *bene-*

This Latin root means "well," "good," "helpful." It is the basic element of many everyday words.

a. *benefit* comes from *bene-* plus "fit," which derives from a Latin word meaning "to make," "to do." A *benefit* is an act of kindness, a good deed, "anything that promotes well-being." The auction was held for the *benefit* of our church. We hope to *benefit* from your advice.

b. *beneficial* derives from the same elements as "benefit," plus the suffix *-ial*. *Beneficial* means "helpful," "advantageous," "promoting a favorable result." Exercise is considered *beneficial* to one's health.

c. *benediction* is derived from *bene-*, the Latin root *dict-* (meaning "to say," "to speak"), and the suffix *-ion*. A *benediction* is "a blessing," "the act of blessing." The minister closed the exercises with a *benediction*.

d. *benevolent* is made up of *bene-* and Latin *volent-*, meaning "willing." *Benevolent* is used to mean "kindly," "disposed to do good," "charitable." Mother felt *benevolent* toward the homeless children. Some lodges and fraternities are *benevolent* aid societies.

e. *benefactor* comes from *bene-* and a Latin word meaning "someone who does." A *benefactor* is someone who does good deeds, is a supporter of good causes. The art museum needs more *benefactors*. My *benefactor* gave me money for some new clothes.

Other words using the root *bene-* are *beneficiary, benefaction, benefactress, benefice, beneficent, benevolence,* and the related term *benign*.

4. *cred-*

This root means "to trust," "to believe."

a. *credentials* comes from *cred-* and the suffixes *-ent* and *-al*. The word means anything that provides the basis for confidence, belief, and credit. It also means "evidence of authority, rights, and status." Only those with proper *credentials* will be admitted. Her *credentials* as a judge are superior.

b. *credit* comes from *cred-* and has several meanings: trustworthiness, credibility; acknowledgment of having done something creditable; time allowed for payment; confidence in a person's ability to perform or pay; to accept as true. He deserves *credit* for his effort. His *credit* at the bank is in doubt. The judge did not *credit* my account of the accident.

  c. *accredit* means "to give credit to," "to certify," "to believe." Our institution is *accredited* by the state board of education.

  d. *discredit* means "not to believe," not to accept." Your action is a *discredit* to you and to your family. The prosecutor *discredited* everything the witness said.

Other words built upon the root *cred-* are *creditable, creditor, credible, credulous, credibility, incredulous, incredible,* and *incredibility.* You can guess the meanings of these words, but if you are in any doubt, check your dictionary.

  5. *dict-*

The root *dict-* means "to speak," "to say."

  a. *diction* means "the style of speaking or writing dependent upon a choice of words." The speaker was noted for his excellent *diction. Diction* varies from region to region in this country.

  b. *dictum* means "a saying," "an assertion," "a maxim," "a pronouncement." The governor's *dictum* stopped the riot. There were many *dictums* (or *dicta*) in *Poor Richard's Almanac.*

  c. *edict* means "a decree," "a proclamation," "a command." The queen issued an *edict* banning public gatherings. A sovereign's *edict* cannot be ignored.

  d. *contradict* means "to deny," "to speak contrary to a statement," "to refute." His actions *contradict* his principles. The witness *contradicted* her earlier testimony.

  e. *dictate* means "to say or read aloud," "to command with authority." She will *dictate* many letters today. Congress *dictated* changes in the income tax laws.

Other words involving *dict-* are *addict, predict, contradictory, dictation, dictionary, dictatorial, predictable, Dictaphone, dictatorship.*

6. *fac-*

This Latin root means "to make," "to do." Also spelled *fic-*, *fact-*, and *fect-*, this root is one of the most widely used of all roots in English.

a. *manufacture* comes from *fact-*, the Latin root *manu-* (meaning "hand"), and the suffix *-ure*. Originally, *manufacture* meant "making by hand" but has come to mean the making of goods and products by machinery or manual labor. *Manufacture* also means "to invent," "to make up," "to fabricate." Sewing machines are *manufactured* in that building. He was driving too fast and had to *manufacture* an excuse for the accident.

b. *fiction* means "something imagined, invented, or feigned." The word is usually applied to "made-up" novels, plays, stories, and narrative poems. In this sense it means "not real," "imaginary." Is this book considered fact or *fiction?* Your explanation for the mistake is pure *fiction*.

c. *factitious* means "artificial," "contrived," "not spontaneous or natural." Her report of activities seems *factitious* to me.

d. *facile* means "easily done," "unconstrained," "affable," "agreeable." His ideas seem weak to me, but he is a *facile* speaker. *Facile* people are pleasant but often boring.

e. *infect* means "to contaminate," "to affect with a disease," "to influence." The enemy tried to *infect* the air with poison gas. His good humor *infected* the audience.

These are among the many words built on this root: *affect, effect, facility, fictional, infectious, infection, efficient, affection, proficiency, factual, factor, defect, defection, factory, perfect, defective*.

7. *fer-*

This root means "to carry," "to bring." It appears in scores of words, among them:

a. *transfer*, from the Latin *trans-* ("across") and *fer-*, means "to move from one place to another," "to cause to pass from one person to another." He will have to *transfer* his office from Chicago to Atlanta. Please *transfer* your ownership of the car to your husband.

b. *conference* means "a meeting for discussion," "a bringing together for consultation." The *conference* of executives is scheduled for next Thursday.

c. *fertile* means "capable of bearing and producing," "bringing to life," "productive." This is *fertile* soil. You have a *fertile* imagination.

d. *differ* comes from the Latin *dif-* ("apart") and *fer-*. The word means "to disagree," "to be at variance with." Do you always have to *differ* with my ideas?

e. *offer* comes from a Latin prefix meaning "before" and *-fer*. "To offer" is to present for acceptance or rejection, "to proffer." An *offer* is something proposed or presented. I'd like to *offer* a proposal. Our *offer* for the house was not accepted.

Other words formed from this root include *confer, offering, transferable, suffer, preference, referendum, offertory, defer, prefer, refer, reference.*

8. *gen-*

The root *gen-* has several applications but usually appears in words meaning "to give birth to," "to produce," "to cause."

a. *genesis* means "an origin," "creation," "beginning." *Genesis*, the first book in the Bible, gives a story of creation. What was the *genesis* of your fear of the dark?

b. *generate* means "to cause to be," "to bring into existence," "to reproduce." This dynamo *generates* electricity for most of that end of town. Our professor *generates* one idea after another.

c. *homogenize* means "to bring into being by blending unlike elements," "to make parts of the same kind." Dairymen *homogenize* milk by breaking up fat globules.

d. *genocide* means "the extermination of a racial or national group." The word is formed from *gen-* ("race") and *-cide* ("killer"). Hitler's efforts at *genocide* eventually met with failure.

e. *genital* comes from *genit-* ("to give birth to") and the suffix *-al* ("pertaining to"). *Genital* means "pertaining to the sexual organs and birth-giving process." That physician specializes in *genital* disorders.

Study your dictionary until you have mastered these additional words built on the root *gen-*: *oxygen, hydrogen, ingenious, ingenuity, congenital, genuine, congenial, ingenuous, genial, progenitor.*

9. *grav-*
This Latin root means "heavy," "weighty."

a. *gravity* comes from *grav-* and the suffix *-ity*, meaning "the state or quality of." *Gravity* suggests both "heaviness" and "the force of attraction by which terrestrial bodies tend to fall toward the center of the earth." Don't you feel the force of *gravity* from this height?

b. *grave* means "serious," "weighty," "important," and "critical." She is suffering from a *grave* illness. This *grave* problem must be settled in court. The expression on your face is *grave*.

c. *gravamen* means the part of an accusation that weighs most heavily against the accused, and a grievance. The essential part of this *gravamen* is based on a lie. Why not take the *gravamen* that has arisen to a court of law?

d. *aggravate* means "to make worse," "to make more of a burden or trouble." His anxiety was *aggravated* by a heavy cold.

e. *gravitate* means "to move in response to gravity," "to sink," "to move downward." It also means "to be attracted to," as if by force. The boy and girl quickly *gravitated* toward each other.

10. *jac-*
This root means "to throw," "to be thrown down." The root is also spelled *ject*.

a. *reject* means "to refuse to accept, recognize, or make use of." It also means "to deny," "to refuse to consider," and "to throw away." The machine will *reject* faulty tokens. If you wish to marry you had better not *reject* every proposal you get.

b. *trajectory* means "the path of a moving body," and, in geometry, means a curve that cuts all of a family of surfaces at the same angle. Literally, the word means "to throw across," from *trans-* ("across") and *ject-* ("throw"). What is the *trajectory* of that shooting star?

c. *inject* means "to place, throw, or shoot something into something else." It also means "to introduce." The nurse *injected* morphine into the arm of the victim. The senator *injected* some irony into his remarks.

d. *project* means "to throw forward," "to put forth," "to hurl," "to impel." Try to *project* your voice to the rear of the auditorium. As a noun, *project* means "a plan," "something proposed." The city fathers approved the *project*.

e. *projector* refers to "a machine for throwing an image onto a screen," "a device for projecting a beam of light," and "someone who devises plans." We'll see the whole movie when the *projector* is repaired. Who was the *projector* of that idea?

Other words built on this root are *adjective, projection, abject, dejection, interjection, projectile, object, projectionist, subject, ejaculate, adjacent.*

11. *loqu-*
   This Latin root, also appearing as *loc-* and *locut-*, means "to speak," "to utter."

a. *loquacious* means "talkative," "garrulous," "verbose," "glib." The elderly men in front of the town hall are a *loquacious* lot.

b. *ventriloquist* applies to a person who can originate speech and other sounds so that they appear to

come from a source other than the speaker. It is
made up of Latin *ventri-* and *loqu-* plus the suffix
-ist. Literally, the word means "belly speaker." This
popular *ventriloquist* uses a wooden dummy.

c. *colloquial* comes from *col-* ("together"), *loqui-* ("to
speak"), and *-al* ("pertaining to"). The word means
"informal," since it applies to people speaking together in conversational style. The speaker talked
in a *colloquial* style. Some *colloquialisms* are not
suitable for formal writing.

d. *elocution* refers to a person's manner of speaking
and also to the practice and study of oral speech. It
is closely related to *eloquent*, which means "speaking out fully," "speaking fluently and gracefully."
The minister is an *eloquent* speaker. Perhaps he
studied *elocution* in college.

e. *interlocutor* means "a partner in a dialogue," "a
performer in a minstrel show." The judge acted as
an *interlocutor* as he tried to get facts from all the
witnesses.

12. *mit-*

Mit- and its variant, *miss-*, mean "to send," "to let go."

a. *commit* literally means "to send together," but in
everyday use it means "to perform," "to place in
trust," and "to consign." Please *commit* these in-
structions to memory. The document was
committed to the fire.

b. *omit* literally means "to send forward," but is used
to mean "fail to include," "to leave out something,"
"to let go." Don't *omit* bacon from your shopping
list. By mistake I *omitted* a word from the sentence.

c. *missile* means "something that can be let go," "be
sent," and can be applied to a rock, a snowball, an
arrow, a bullet, or a rocket. Do you remember the
name of the first manned *missile*?

d. *missionary* means "one who is sent on a mission,

usually to do charitable, religious, or medical
work." Her parents were *missionaries* in China.

  e. *permit* means "to send" or "let something
      through" and has current meanings of "allow," "to
      consent to," and "authorize." He has a learner's
      permit. No standing or parking is *permitted* on
      this street.

Other words built on a *mit-*, *miss-* root include *emit*, *dismiss*,
omission, *transmit*, *transmitted*, *transmission*, *remit*, *remission*,
missive, *intermittent*, *emissary*.

 13. *pend-*
      This root, also appearing as *pens-*, has various mean-
      ings: "to hang," "to pay," "to weigh."

  a. *suspend* comes from the prefix *sus-* ("under") and
      pens- ("to hang"). Literally meaning "to hang un-
      der," *suspend* is now used to mean "to defer action
      or plans," "to deny a privilege," "to hang from a
      support." We will have to *suspend* payments on the
      mortgage. The lantern is *suspended* from a tree
      limb.

  b. *pensive* means "engaged in deep thought," "sus-
      pended in troubled revery." *Pensive* persons always
      weigh their problems seriously.

  c. *pendulum* refers to a mass hung from a fixed sup-
      port and to something that swings back and forth
      from one course or one idea or opinion. The *pen-
      dulum* of public opinion is often difficult to follow.

  d. *depend* originally meant "to hang down," but now
      means "to rely on," "to trust," "to be assured." I'll
      have to *depend* on you for a place to stay. Our pic-
      nic plans *depend* on the weather.

  e. *append* means "to add as a supplement," "to at-
      tach," "to fix to." He *appended* a codicil to his will.
      I'd like to *append* a note to your letter.

Other *pend-*, *pens-* words: *appendage*, *appendant*, *suspend-
ers*, *dependable*, *dependence*, *dispense*, *recompense*, *suspense*,

indispensable, dispensary, expendable, expenditure, compensate, compensation, pendulous, pending.

14. *ple-, plet-*
    This root, in both spellings, means "to fill."
    a. *complete* means "filled thoroughly," "full," "entire," "whole," "having all necessary parts." She ran the *complete* course. I have *completed* all the books on that shelf.
    b. *replete* literally means "filled again" and is used to mean "plentifully supplied," "abounding," "filled to satiation." After that huge meal I feel *replete*. This menu is *replete* with all necessary vitamins.
    c. *deplete* comes from a Latin prefix meaning "not" and *plet-*. The word means "not to fill" and is used to mean "lessening by use or waste," "to use up." If you don't stop spending you will soon *deplete* your funds. My sister's strength was *depleted* by fever.
    d. *plethora* means "superabundant," "filled up," "an excess." You will soon receive a *plethora* of advice. No one ever has a *plethora* of love or money.
    e. *plenitude* means "abundance," "the condition of being full, ample or complete." The table was laden with a *plenitude* of rich foods.

Other *ple-, plet-* words: *implement, depletion, plenteous, implementation, plenty, plenary, plentiful.*

15. *port-*
    The root *port-* means "to carry."
    a. *portable* comes from *port-* and the suffix *-able*, meaning "capable of doing and being." *Portable* refers to something that is capable of being moved or carried. She bought a *portable* television set. This lightweight canoe is easily *portable*.
    b. *portage* means "the carrying of supplies and boats overland between two waterways," "a route or track by which carrying is done," and "to transport

by portage." The *portage* above the falls extends
for 200 yards. You will need to *portage* food for a
three-week stay.

c. *transportation* means "the act of carrying or con-
veying from one place to another." It also means "a
conveyance," "a means of transport." All buses are
in the *transportation* business.

d. *export* comes from the prefix *ex-*, meaning "out,"
and *port-*. *Export* means "to send or carry abroad,
especially for sale or trade." This country *exports*
much grain to Asia. What is the major *export* of
Chile?

e. *import* comes from the Latin prefix *im-* ("in") and
port-. *Import* means "to bring or carry in from an
outside source." A major *import* of this country is
natural rubber. Russia seems to need to *import*
grain every year.

Other *port-* words include *report, portal, deport, deportee,
transport, disport, porter, support, reporter, supporter.*

16. *rupt-*
This root means "to break," "to burst."

a. *disrupt* comes from the prefix *dis-* ("apart") and
rupt-. The word means not only "to break," "to
burst," but also "to throw into confusion," "to upset
the order of." The hecklers *disrupted* the scheduled
meeting. A serious accident *disrupted* our plans for
the trip.

b. *abrupt* means "sudden," "unexpectedly," "cut or
broken off short." Your comments are both rude
and *abrupt*.

c. *interrupt* means "to break the uniformity or conti-
nuity of some action," "to hinder or stop something," "to break in upon some act or speech." The
movie was *interrupted* when the film broke. Our
plans were *interrupted* by a shortage of money.

d. *erupt* means "to force out," "to release suddenly,"

"to explode," "to become violently active." That
volcano will soon *erupt*. The meeting *erupted* into
a near riot.

e. *rupture*, as a verb, means "to break apart or break
open." As a noun, *rupture* means "a bursting," "a
breaking." Bankruptcy *ruptured* all our plans. The
rupture between Syria and Israel was serious.

Other *rupt-* words include *eruption, corrupt, corruption, disruption, disruptive.*

17. *scrib-*
This root, which also appears as *script-*, means "to
write."

a. *manuscript* means "a book, document, or other
composition written by hand." Although *manuscript* literally means "handwritten," it is commonly
used to refer to copy (material) submitted for printing or other use whether the copy is handwritten or
typewritten. Your *manuscript* is neatly typed. The
author lost his *manuscript* on a bus.

b. *inscription* means "the wording on a coin or
medal," "an epitaph," "the dedication of a book or
other work of art." The *inscription* on her tombstone is "She kept the faith."

c. *prescribe* is built on *scribe-* and the prefix *pre-*. The
word has more than one meaning: "to set down as a
rule"; "to order or ordain"; "to recommend a treatment or remedy"; "to establish rules or regulations." The physician *prescribed* no remedy for my
uncle. The *prescribed* dress for the party is "formal."

d. *describe* is introduced by the prefix *de-* (meaning
"down"). It is used to mean "to give an account of
some action," "to transmit an image or impression," and "to trace or draw." When you *describe*
someone you write down or speak the words that
draw a picture. The teacher told us to *describe* a
typical classroom.

e. *subscribe* comes from word elements meaning "to write beneath." It is used to mean "to sign," "to pledge or contribute," "to express approval or consent." I do not *subscribe* to your proposal. Why do you *subscribe* to that magazine?

Other *scribe-, script-* words include *transcribe, inscribe, prescribe, ascribe, conscript, conscription, circumscribe, scribble, Scripture, script.*

18. *tract-*
This root means "to pull," "to draw," "to drag."
a. *tractable* means "easily managed or controlled," "not difficult to pull or drag into line," "easily handled or worked." Her favorite horse is unusually *tractable.* Most good medical students are *tractable.*
b. *extract* literally means "to pull out," but it has several associated meanings: "to draw forth forcibly"; "to obtain despite resistance"; "to remove for consideration or study"; "to copy a passage from a book or other source." This machine *extracts* syrup from cane. An exodontist is a dentist who *extracts* teeth. Please read me that *extract* again. The cake tasted of vanilla *extract.*
c. *detract* means "to diminish," "to take a desirable part of." Your clothes *detract* from your chances for a job. Loud talk by others *detracted* from our enjoyment of the play.
d. *contract* (to draw together) means "to establish or settle by agreement," "to shrink," "to shorten," and, as a noun, means "an agreement," "a paper or document detailing an agreement." The *contract* is fair and complete. The medicine made the pupils of his eyes seem to *contract.*
e. *distract* literally means "to draw away" and is regularly used to mean "to bewilder," "to confuse," "to divert mind or attention." Don't let your love for

him *distract* you. Noises from the pneumatic drill *distracted* the listeners at the musical.

Other *tract-* words: *tractor, extraction, attraction, attractive, contraction, contractor, contractual, detractor, distraction, extraction, protract, retract, tract, traction, subtract, subtraction.*

19. *ven-*

This root, which also appears as *vent-*, means "to come," "to move toward."

a. *event,* which literally means "to come out," "to happen," is used for "an occurrence, experience, or incident." *Event* also means the actual outcome or final result of something and "one of the items in a program of entertainment or sports." The election of 1800 was an important *event.* My solo was the last *event* on the program.

b. *convention* means "a coming together," "an assembly," "an agreement dealing with a specific subject," "a device or technique." This *convention* was well attended. There are many *conventions* for the treatment of prisoners of war.

c. *revenue* means "a collection of funds," "the yield from property," "the income of a government." This state collects millions of dollars of *revenue* from sales taxes.

d. *circumvent* means "to get around something," "to come around," "to overcome," "to avoid." We tried to *circumvent* the parking regulations. Take some aspirin and *circumvent* a cold.

e. *intervene* means "to come between," "to appear to lie between two things," "to hinder," "to modify." The referee *intervened* in the players' fight. Please don't try to *intervene* in our dispute.

Other *ven-, vent-* words: *invent, prevent, prevention, preventive, advent, adventure, venturesome, venture, inventive, inventor, eventful, eventuality, eventual, convenient, convenience, conventional, unconventional.*

20. *voc-*

This Latin root (also appearing as *vok-* and *voke-*)
means both "voice" and "to call."

a. *vocal* means "of or pertaining to the voice"; "having
a voice capable of emitting sound"; "resounding
with speech." The crew's displeasure was both
physical and *vocal*. He was *vocal* in favor of his
friend.

b. *invoke* means "to call upon his help," "to appeal
to," "to petition." The defendant *invoked* the Fifth
Amendment. The rabbi *invoked* God's blessing on
the assembly.

c. *vociferous* means "making an outcry," "clamorous,"
"characterized by loudness." The mob was *vociferous* in its demands.

d. *vocation* means "a calling," "an urge to undertake a
line of work to which one feels called," "an occupation or profession." His law practice is his *vocation*,
but his *avocation* is gardening.

e. *revoke* means "to recall," "to annul or avoid by recalling," "to fail to follow suit." Our leader *revoked*
her permission for us to leave. When I *revoked*
during the bridge game my partner was furious.

Other *voc-*, *vok-*, *voke-* words: *evoke, vocalist, vocalize, vociferate, vocabulary, provoke, provocation, provocative, irrevocable, revocation.*

7

USE A DICTIONARY:

COMBINING FORMS

A *combining form* is a word element that combines other words, or parts of words, to form compounds. Examples are "logy" as in *psychology,* "micro" as in *microscope,* and "Sino" as in *Sinophile* (one friendly to the Chinese) or *Sino-Tibetan. Graph,* for example, although it is a word by itself, appears frequently as a combining form in such words as "photography," "geography," and "lithography."

Experts differ in the ways in which they classify combining forms, prefixes, roots, and suffixes. What one writer on language would call a root, another would term a combining form or suffix. Even so, knowing the meanings and applications of forms like the following, however you choose to call them, will greatly increase your spelling ability.

1. *anima* means "life," "breath."

   animation   animate   animalism
   animal   inanimate   animadvert

2. *aqua* means "water."

   aquarium   aquacade   aquifer
   aqueduct   aquamarine   aqualung

3. *bios* means "life."

   biopsy   bioplasm   biometrics
   bionics   biosphere   biosynthesis

4. *culpa* means "fault," "negligence."

culprit	culpability	culpableness
culpable	culpably	culpatory

5. *domus* means "house," "home."

domicile	domesticate	domesticity
domestic	domesticable	domestication

6. *ego* means "I."

egoism	egocentric	egomania
egotism	egoist	egotist

7. *facilis* means "easy."

facile	facilitate	facilitation
facility	facilely	facileness

8. *gramma* means "letter."

grammar	grammarian	grammalogue
grammatical	grammarless	grammaticism

9. *lex* means "law."

lawyer	lawful	lawmaker
legal	lawless	legality

10. *liber* means "book."

library	libretti	librarian
libretto	libriform	librettist

11. *locus* means "place."

locality	location	locate
local	locator	locative

12. *navis* means "ship."

navigate	navy	navigation
naval	navigable	navigator

13. *opus* means "work."

operation	operational	operative
opera	operate	operator

14. *populus* means "people."

population	populace	populate
popularity	populous	popularize

15. *sanctus* means "holy."

sanctuary	sanctity	sanctimonious
sanctify	sanctifier	sanction

16. *sophia* means "wisdom."

sophisticated	sophism	sophomore
sophistry	philosophy	sophist

17. *spectro* means "light."

spectrum	spectroscope	spectrogram
spectroscopy	spectroscopic	spectrograph

18. *tactus* means "quiet," "silence."

tacit	taciturnly	tacitly
taciturn	taciturnity	tacitness

19. *thermo* means "heat."

thermometer	thermal	thermochemistry
thermostat	isotherm	thermodynamics

20. *vita* means "life."

vitamin	vitality	vitals
vital	vitalize	vitally

Give the meaning of each of these combining forms. Then use each form in a sentence with the formed words correctly spelled.

1. aristos	5. hostis	9. plus, pluris
2. beatus	6. mater	10. Sino
3. causa	7. pedi	11. umbra
4. decem	8. petra	

8

USE A DICTIONARY:

PREFIXES

Prefixes are syllables added to the beginnings of words to alter or modify their meanings or, occasionally, to form entirely new words. For example, we add the prefix *mis-* to the word *spell* and form *misspell*.

Prefixes

a-	not	amoral, anonymous
ad-	to, against	adverse, adjective
ambi-	around, both	ambiguous, ambidextrous
ante-	before	antedate, anteroom
anti-	opposite	antisocial, antiwar
audio-	hearing	audiovisual, audition
auto-	self, same	autograph, autobiography
bene-	well, good	beneficial, benefit
bio-	life	biography, biology
circum-	about, around	circumstance, circumflex
co-	complement of	comaker, co-signer
col-	together	collateral, collection
com-	in association	combine, compare
de-	away, down, from	demerit, degrade
dis-	apart, not, away	disbar, disability
ec- (ex-)	from, out of	eccentric, exhale
en- (em-)	in, on, into	enact, empower
epi-	upon, before	epigram, epilogue
ex-	out of, from	exclaim, excommunicate

extra-	beyond, without	extrajudicial, extrasensory
hemi-	half	hemisphere, hemiplegia
hyper-	beyond the ordinary	hypercritical, hypersensitive
il-	not	illogical, illegitimate
im-	opposed, negative	immoral, imbalance
inter-	among, between	interdepartmental, intercollegiate
intra-	within	intramural, intravenous
ir-	not, opposed	irreligious, irreducible
meta-	along with, among	metaphysics, metamorphism
mono-	one, alone	monochrome, monologue
neo-	new, recent	neophyte, neolithic
para-	beside	paragraph, parachute
per-	through, thoroughly	pervert, perfect
peri-	about, beyond	perimeter, perigee
poly-	marry	polygon, polysyllable
post-	behind, after	postscript, postgraduate
pro-	for, forward	proclivity, proceed
pseudo-	false	pseudoclassic, pseudonym
re-	backward, again	revert, return
retro-	backward	retrogress, retroactive
semi-	half	semidetached, semicolon
super-	above, beyond	supernatural, supersensitive
syn-	together, with	synthesis, syndrome
tel- (tele-)	distant	telegraph, telecast
trans-	across, beyond	transcend, transmit
ultra-	beyond, in excess of	ultraviolet, ultrasonic
un-	not, reverse of	unfair, unbend

This is a brief list of prefixes, but they appear in a large number of misspelled words. Here are notes on the spelling of words containing a few of these prefixes:

Ad-

This prefix alters its form according to the root word to which it is attached. For example, before a root beginning *sc* or *sp*, the *d* is dropped, as in *ascent* and *aspire*. Before such letters as *c, f, g, l, n, p,* and *t,* the *d* in *ad-* is assimilated (becomes the same as the following letter): *accommodate, affix, aggression, allegation, announce, appoint, attend.*

Ante-, anti-

The first of these prefixes is of Latin origin and means "before" or "prior." *Anti-* is from Greek and means "opposite" or "against." Note these different spellings:

antebellum (before the war)
antemeridian (before noon; A.M.)
ante mortem (before death)
anteroom (room before)
antetype (an earlier form)
antiaircraft (defense against aircraft)
antibiotic (defense against bacteria)
anticlimax (contrast to preceding rise in action)
antifreeze (against freezing)
antiseptic (against infection)

De-, dis-

These prefixes will cause spelling problems when you don't distinguish clearly between root words beginning with *s* and the prefixes themselves. Note these spellings:

describe (write down) *de + scribe*
despoil (strip down) *de + spoil*
dissemble (disguise) *dis + semble*
dissimilar (unlike) *dis + similar*

Remember: only about thirty common words begin with *diss-* but ten times as many begin with *dis-*. Only three fairly common words (and their derivatives) begin with *dys-: dysentery, dyspepsia, dystrophy* (as in "muscular dystrophy").

A simple rule: when the prefixes *dis-* and *mis-* are added to a *root* word beginning with *s*, neither *s* should be omitted: *dissatisfied, misstep.* When they are added to roots not beginning with an *s*, use only one *s: disappear, misfortune.*

Inter-

This prefix meaning "between" is frequently confused with *intra-*, which means "inside," "within."

interfere (carry between)
intercollegiate (between colleges)
interstate (between, among states)
intramural (within the walls)
intrastate (within a state)
intravenous (within a vein, veins)

Un-

When this prefix is added to a root word beginning with *n*, neither *n* is omitted:

unnamed	unnegotiable	unnumbered
unnatural	unnoted	unnurtured
unnecessary	unnoticeable	
unneeded	unnoticed	

9

USE A DICTIONARY:

SUFFIXES

A suffix is an element that is placed after a word or word root to make a term of different use or meaning. For example, the suffix *-age* has a general meaning of "belonging to." *Postage* (*post* plus *age*) has to do with a series of stations along a route that receive and send mail. With this sense of *-age* in mind, words such as *coinage, fruitage, spoilage*, and *bondage* become clear. Common suffixes include these:

-ana	Americana, collegiana	*-let*	bracelet, ringlet
-ance	connivance, nonchalance	*-like*	lifelike, childlike
-dom	kingdom, freedom	*-logy*	trilogy, theology
-er	loiterer, embezzler	*-ness*	kindness, preparedness
-fold	manifold, twofold	*-phone*	telephone, megaphone
-ful	beautiful, harmful	*-polis*	metropolis, megalopolis
-graph	monograph, lithograph	*-ship*	friendship, statesmanship
-hood	childhood, priesthood	*-some*	twosome, quarrelsome
-ice	apprentice, novice	*-ward*	toward, afterward
-ish	British, girlish	*-ways*	always, sideways
-ism	barbarism, plagiarism	*-wise*	clockwise, sidewise
-ity	civility, nobility	*-y*	dreamy, infamy

There are only eight suffix groups which cause major spelling problems. Within each group are many words that give trouble, some of the most often misspelled words in the language. Here is a brief discussion of each of the eight groups.

-Able, -Ible

Even excellent spellers have occasional difficulties with these endings; they can unhesitatingly spell most words having one or the other of these suffixes, but once in a while they, too, must seek out their dictionaries.

With this spelling problem the best advice is to "Stop and Look." (It won't do any good to "listen," for pronunciation is identical.) To an efficient speller a word that should end in *-ible* doesn't "look right" when it ends in *-able*. He is relying entirely on his visual image of the correct spelling.

But for those whose visual recall is deficient, there *are* some guiding principles concerning *-able* and *-ible*. They are fairly easy to learn and involve no more exceptions than most rules for spelling. There are five group forms for *-able*, the same number for *-ible*.

-Able

1. The ending should usually be *-able* if the base (root) is a full word: *eat* + *able*.

Fortunately, many of our most familiar, most used words add *-able* to form adjectives. Note that if you drop *-able* from each of the following, you are left with a *complete* word:

acceptable	dependable	peaceable
available	detectable	perishable
avoidable	detestable	predictable
breakable	discreditable	presentable
changeable	drinkable	profitable
comfortable	fashionable	readable
commendable	favorable	seasonable
companionable	laughable	taxable
considerable	noticeable	thinkable
creditable	passable	workable

2. The ending should usually be *-able* if the base is a full word except for lacking a final *e: desire* + *able* = *desirable*.

Fortunately, this group of -*able* words is not nearly so large as the preceding one. The following words illustrate the basic principle:

believable	excitable	presumable
debatable	excusable	sizable
deplorable	likable	usable
describable	lovable	valuable
desirable	pleasurable	

3. The ending should usually be -*able* if the base ends in *i* (the original word may have ended in *y*): *enviable*.

This principle of spelling makes more sense than most spelling "rules." If it were not followed we would have a double *i* (*ii*), an unusual combination even in our weird spelling system.

appreciable	enviable	satisfiable
classifiable	justifiable	sociable
dutiable	reliable	

4. The ending should usually be -*able* if the base has other forms with the sound of long *a*: *demonstrate*, *demonstrable*.

This principle will be helpful only if you actually sound out another form (or forms) of the root word to see whether it has (or they have) the long *a* sound: *abominate*, *abominable; estimate*, *estimable*, etc.

delectable	inflammable	inviolable
durable	inimitable	irreparable
flammable	innumerable	irritable
impenetrable	inseparable	reparable
impregnable	intolerable	

5. The ending should usually be -*able* if the base ends in hard *c* or hard *g*.

Hard *c* is sounded like the *c* in *cat;* hard *g* has the sound of *g* in *get*. The following words illustrate this principle:

amicable	implacable	irrevocable
applicable	indefatigable	revocable
despicable	navigable	
explicable	practicable	

These five principles cover most of the fairly common words which have endings in *-able*. But there are a few exceptions. If you wish to be able to spell all words ending with *-able*, then study the following by some other method suggested in this book; rules won't help much:

affable	ineffable	palpable
arable	inevitable	portable
culpable	inscrutable	potable
equitable	insuperable	probable
formidable	malleable	unconscionable
indomitable	memorable	vulnerable

-Ible

1. The ending should usually be *-ible* if the base is *not* a full word.

Contrast this principle with Number 1 under *-Able* (above). If the base is a complete word, we then add *-able: mail + able = mailable.* If the base is not a complete word, we add *-ible: ris + ible = risible,* and *poss + ible = possible.*

audible	feasible	negligible
combustible	horrible	ostensible
compatible	incorrigible	plausible
credible	indelible	tangible
dirigible	infallible	terrible
divisible	intelligible	visible
edible	irascible	

2. The ending should usually be *-ible* if the base ends in *-ns: respons + ible = responsible.*

These words illustrate this spelling principle:

comprehensible	insensible	reprehensible
defensible	irresponsible	responsible
incomprehensible	ostensible	sensible
indefensible		

3. The ending should usually be *-ible* if the base ends in *-miss: admiss + ible = admissible.*

Comparatively few words belong in this category. Here are several examples:

dismissible	permissible	transmissible
omissible	remissible	

With roots not ending in *-miss*, but closely related, are such words with *-ible* endings as *accessible, compressible, irrepressible,* and *possible* (which also fits under Group 1 above).

4. The ending should usually be *-ible* if *-ion* can be added to the base without intervening letters: *collect, collection, collectible.*

Quite a few words create such new forms by the immediate (nothing coming between) addition of *-ion.* All such words form adjectives ending in *-ible*; here are a few samples:

accessible	contractible	inexhaustible
affectible	convertible	perfectible
collectible	corruptible	reversible
connectible	digestible	suggestible

You should note that this rule is tricky: if *-ion* cannot be added to the root immediately (without intervening letters), the *-able* ending is more likely as in *present, presentation, presentable.*

5. The ending should usually be *-ible* if the base ends in soft *c* or soft *g.*

This principle should be compared with Number 5 under *-Able.* A soft *c* sounds like an *s* (force); a soft *g* sounds like a *j* (tangent). The following words contain a soft *c* or a soft *g*. Also note that, with few exceptions, the roots are not complete words.

conducible	incorrigible	negligible
convincible	intangible	producible
deducible	intelligible	reducible
eligible	invincible	seducible
forcible	irascible	
illegible	legible	

Just as there are a few exceptions to the rules for *-able* endings (see page 99), so are there for words ending in *-ible*. The commonly used words which are exceptions are not numerous. Among those words which, by rule, should end in *-able* but do not are the following:

collapsible	flexible	irresistible
contemptible	gullible	resistible
discernible	inflexible	

The following words merit careful study because each is an exception to the principles discussed above:

correctable	dispensable	predictable
detectable	indispensable	

-Ally, -Ly

These two suffixes are often confused by spellers with inadequate visual memories. Because these endings appear so often in commonly used words, they account for large numbers of misspellings. The same advice applies: when in doubt, consult your dictionary.

Perhaps these basic principles concerning *-ly* will also be helpful:

1. The suffix *-ly* is used to form an adverb from an adjective: *poor* + *ly* = *poorly*. If the adjective ends in *-l*, *-ly* is tacked on to the complete root, thus producing an *-lly* ending.

Here is a list of frequently used, and occasionally misspelled, adverbs:

accidentally	fundamentally	personally
actually	generally	physically
annually	incidentally	practically
continually	individually	really
coolly	intentionally	skillfully
cruelly	literally	successfully
especially	logically	truthfully
exceptionally	morally	universally
finally	naturally	unusually
fully	occasionally	usually

2. The suffix -*ly* is added to basic words ending in silent *e*, and the *e* is retained.

absolutely	immediately	severely
completely	infinitely	sincerely
entirely	scarcely	

3. If an adjective ends in -*ic*, its adverbial form ends in -*ally*.

This is a simple, clear rule with only one exception: *publicly*. This word you must simply fix in your visual memory. Here are examples of adverbs formed from adjectives with -*ic* endings:

academically	emphatically	scholastically
artistically	fantastically	systematically
automatically	grammatically	
basically	lyrically	

The following adverbs do not completely follow the principles just enumerated. Fix them in your visual memory:

duly	possibly	wholly
incredibly	terribly	
only	truly	

-Ance, -Ence

The suffixes *-ance* and *-ence* are added to root words (verbs) to form nouns: *attend, attendance; prefer, preference.*

With one exception, to be noted below, there is no uniform guiding principle to your choice of *-ance* or *-ence*. Here again, correct pronunciation is of no help. True, if you know the conjugation of Latin verbs you can form a helpful rule, but so few of us do know Latin that it's useless to state the principle. Your only safe procedure is to consult your dictionary and try to form good visual images of *-ance* and *-ence* words.

One helpful principle, and one only, is this: if a verb ends in *r* preceded by a vowel and is accented on the last syllable, it forms its noun with *-ence:*

abhorrence	deference	preference
coherence	inference	recurrence
concurrence	interference	reference
conference	occurrence	transference

Here are lists of often misspelled words ending in *-ance* and *-ence*. Study each until you have a total recall of its appearance.

Frequently Misspelled -Ance Words

abeyance	continuance	observance
abundance	contrivance	performance
acceptance	defiance	perseverance
acquaintance	deliverance	radiance
admittance	distance	relevance
allegiance	elegance	reliance
alliance	endurance	remembrance
allowance	entrance	remittance
ambulance	furtherance	repentance
annoyance	grievance	resistance
appearance	guidance	significance
arrogance	instance	substance
assurance	insurance	sustenance
attendance	irrelevance	temperance
balance	maintenance	tolerance
brilliance	nuisance	vengeance

Frequently Misspelled *-Ence* Words

absence	difference	obedience
abstinence	eminence	patience
audience	essence	permanence
circumference	evidence	preference
coherence	excellence	presence
coincidence	existence	prominence
competence	experience	prudence
conference	impudence	reference
confidence	incidence	residence
conscience	inference	reverence
convenience	influence	sentence
correspondence	innocence	silence
deference	insistence	subsistence
dependence	interference	violence

-Ar, -Er, -Or

The suffixes *-ar*, *-er*, and *-or* have various origins, functions, and meanings. Their most common shared meaning denotes an actor, a doer, "one who." Many thousands of English words end in *-ar*, *-er*, and *-or*, but here again accurate pronunciation is little aid in spelling; furthermore, no rules or principles are applicable to their correct spelling. Consult your dictionary; try to form accurate visual images.

Following are lists of *-ar*, *-er*, and *-or* words often misspelled. In not every word is the ending a true suffix, but correct spelling is now your objective, not a study of word origins or of word building.

Frequently Misspelled Words Ending in *-Ar*

altar	caterpillar	curricular
angular	cedar	dollar
beggar	cellar	familiar
burglar	circular	grammar
calendar	collar	hangar

insular	particular	similar
jugular	peculiar	singular
liar	pillar	spectacular
lunar	polar	sugar
molar	popular	vehicular
muscular	regular	vinegar
nectar	scholar	vulgar

Frequently Misspelled Words Ending in -*Er*

advertiser	defender	minister
adviser	diameter	murder
alter	disaster	observer
announcer	employer	officer
baker	examiner	partner
beginner	foreigner	passenger
believer	haberdasher	prisoner
boarder	jeweler	provider
border	laborer	soldier
boulder	lawyer	teacher
carrier	lecturer	traveler
commissioner	manager	writer
consumer	manufacturer	
debater	messenger	

Frequently Misspelled Words Ending in -*Or*

accelerator	benefactor	debtor
actor	cantor	dictator
administrator	collector	director
aggressor	commentator	distributor
anchor	competitor	doctor
auditor	conqueror	editor
author	contributor	educator
aviator	councilor	elevator
bachelor	counselor	emperor
behavior	creditor	escalator

executor	manor	radiator
factor	minor	sailor
governor	mortgagor	sculptor
harbor	motor	senator
humor	neighbor	suitor
inferior	odor	supervisor
inventor	pastor	tenor
investigator	prior	traitor
janitor	professor	ventilator
legislator	protector	visitor

-Ary, -Ery

This suffix problem is simple. Hundreds and hundreds of English words end in -*ary*. Only a half dozen fairly common words end in -*ery*. Learn the -*ery* words by whatever device presented in this book works best for you. Spell all others with -*ary*. It's as elementary as that.

Here are the words you might use which end in -*ery:*

cemetery	distillery	monastery
confectionery	millinery	stationery

End all other words with -*ary*. You'll be right every time unless you happen to use such a rare word as *philandery*. You will have no spelling problems with the endings of *auxiliary, boundary, dictionary, elementary, honorary, imaginary, library, secretary,* and *voluntary,* and hundreds of other such everyday words.

-Cede, -Ceed, -Sede

These suffixes cause a large number of misspellings because they appear in several common words. But the problem they present is quite simple because so few words are involved. Only twelve words in the language end in this pronunciation, "seed," and not all of these are in common use.

First, only one word in English ends in -*sede: supersede*. It has this ending because of its origin; it comes from the Latin verb *sedeo*, meaning "to sit." As with many other "borrowed" words in English it maintains some connection with its source.

Second, only three of the twelve words ending with the "seed" pronunciation are spelled with *ceed: exceed, proceed,* and *succeed.*

Finally, the eight remaining words end in *cede:*

accede	concede	recede
antecede	intercede	secede
cede	precede	

It won't help with spelling the *-ceed* and *-cede* words to know their origin, but it will help in avoiding a *sede* ending: the eleven *-ceed, -cede* words derive not from *sedeo* (as *supersede* does) but from Latin *cedo,* meaning "to go." Thus, *pre + cede* means "to go or come before"; *inter + cede* means "to go or come between," etc.

-Efy, -Ify

These two suffixes cause much spelling trouble, but here again the problem is simple when it is clearly looked at. Actually, only four words you are likely to use end in *-efy* (and you probably won't use them every day, either). All the remainder, without exception, end in *-ify.*

Therefore, learn these four words by whatever method seems best and spell all others with *-ify:*

liquefy (to make liquid)
putrefy (to make or become rotten)
rarefy (to make or become rare)
stupefy (to make or become insensible)

Also, you should note that words built on these four tend to retain the *e* spelling:

liquefy, liquefies, liquefied, liquefying, liquefaction
putrefy, putrefies, putrefied, putrefying, putrefaction
rarefy, rarefies, rarefied, rarefying, rarefaction
stupefy, stupefies, stupefied, stupefying, stupefaction

-Ise, -Ize, -Yze

Some five hundred fairly common words in our language end in
-ise, *-ize*, and *-yze*. How can one master all these spellings,
especially since correct pronunciation provides no help at all?

Consulting your dictionary will provide some help and so
will training your visual memory until a word you've spelled
with *-ize* just "doesn't look right" if it should end in *-ise*. The
best approach is to isolate the comparatively few words with
-yze and *-ise* and to remember that *-ize* is by far the most
common suffix and that the chances of its being correct are
mathematically excellent.

These are the only four fairly common words in English
ending in *-yze:*

analyze	electrolyze
catalyze	paralyze

Study these four words carefully. Master them by whatever
method seems best: four words are a small matter.

There are no clear rules for choosing between *-ise* and *-ize*
endings. Even though there are well over four hundred words
ending in *-ize*, there are only some thirty or forty with an *-ise*
suffix. (If you live in Great Britain, you will have to cope with a
larger number; several words that the English spell with *-ise*
Americans spell with *-ize*.)

The comparatively few words which end in *-ise* can be grouped
as follows:

1. Combinations with *-cise:*
circumcise	exercise	incise
excise	exorcise	

These *-cise* words are so spelled because they derive from a form,
incisus, of a Latin word meaning "to cut."

2. Combinations with *-guise:*

   disguise   guise

3. Combinations with -*mise:*

compromise	premise
demise	surmise

4. Combinations with -*prise:*

apprise	enterprise	reprise
comprise	emprise	surprise

5. Combinations with -*rise:*

arise	rise	uprise
moonrise	sunrise	

6. Combinations with -*vise:*

advise	improvise	supervise
devise	revise	

These -*vise* words are derived from a form, *visus*, of a Latin word meaning "to see."

7. Combinations with -*wise:*

contrariwise	likewise	sidewise
lengthwise	otherwise	wise

8. Miscellaneous combinations with -*ise:*

advertise	despise	merchandise
chastise	franchise	

This makes a total of less than forty common words ending in -*yze* and -*ise*. All others with this suffixal pronunciation end in -*ize*. Here are a few of the hundreds of words with this ending:

agonize	characterize	plagiarize
apologize	Christianize	pulverize
authorize	civilize	realize
baptize	colonize	recognize
brutalize	criticize	reorganize
cauterize	crystallize	demoralize

economize
equalize
familiarize
fertilize
generalize
harmonize
humanize
jeopardize
legalize
liberalize
localize

scandalize
scrutinize
solemnize
specialize
subsidize
modernize
monopolize
moralize
nationalize
naturalize
neutralize

organize
ostracize
particularize
pasteurize
patronize
philosophize
symbolize
tantalize
utilize
vocalize

10

USE A DICTIONARY:

PLURALS

You can consult your dictionary every time you are unsure about the spelling of a word but, as we have noted, if you do you'll be more a whirling dervish or page-flipper than a writer.

Many people find it fairly easy to spell the singular of a word (meaning "one") but have trouble forming and correctly spelling plurals (meaning "more than one"). This is quite understandable, since many English words form plurals in unusual ways. You can "look it up" in a dictionary when you are puzzled, but a few principles of plural-forming can easily be mastered.

Noun Plurals

1. The plural of most nouns is formed by adding *s* to the singular:

   bed, beds   food, foods
   book, books   hat, hats
   chair, chairs   pot, pots
   cracker, crackers   sheet, sheets
   dog, dogs   table, tables

2. Nouns ending with a sibilant or *s* sound (*ch, sh, s, x, z*) form their plurals by adding *es*:

arch, arches
box, boxes
bush, bushes
buzz, buzzes
church, churches

fox, foxes
loss, losses
mass, masses
tax, taxes
watch, watches

3. Nouns ending in *y* preceded by a consonant usually change *y* to *i* before adding *es:*

activity, activities
category, categories
city, cities
community, communities
fly, flies

forty, forties
library, libraries
quantity, quantities
sky, skies
strawberry, strawberries

4. Nouns ending in *y* preceded by a vowel usually add *s* without changing the final *y:*

alley, alleys
attorney, attorneys
chimney, chimneys
foray, forays
key, keys

money, moneys
monkey, monkeys
toy, toys
turkey, turkeys
valley, valleys

5. Nouns ending in *o* preceded by a vowel add *s* to form their plurals:

cameo, cameos
folio, folios

radio, radios
rodeo, rodeos

6. Nouns ending in *o* preceded by a consonant often add *es* to form the plural:

buffalo, buffaloes
cargo, cargoes
echo, echoes
embargo, embargoes
fresco, frescoes
hero, heroes

mosquito, mosquitoes
Negro, Negroes
potato, potatoes
tomato, tomatoes
tornado, tornadoes
volcano, volcanoes

7. Some nouns ending in *o* preceded by a consonant, including many musical terms, add *s* to form their plurals:

alto, altos	gigolo, gigolos
banjo, banjos	memento, mementos
basso, bassos	piano, pianos
canto, cantos	quarto, quartos
concerto, concertos	silo, silos
contralto, contraltos	solo, solos
dynamo, dynamos	soprano, sopranos
Eskimo, Eskimos	zero, zeros

8. Nouns ending in *f* form their plurals in such variable ways that you should *always* consult your dictionary when in doubt. Nouns ending in *ff* usually add *s*. Most nouns ending in *fe* change *fe* to *ve* and add *s*. The following examples will be sufficient to make you remember the formula: doubt + dictionary = correct spelling:

belief, beliefs	roof, roofs
chief, chiefs	scarf, scarves
grief, griefs	self, selves
half, halfs (or halves)	sheaf, sheaves
handkerchief, hand-	sheriff, sheriffs
kerchiefs	staff, staves (or staffs)
leaf, leaves	tariff, tariffs
life, lives	thief, thieves
loaf, loaves	wife, wives
mischief, mischiefs	wolf, wolves

Compound Nouns

9. Compound nouns ordinarily form the plural by adding *s* or *es* to the important word in the compound.

Sometimes the element considered most important comes first in the compound, sometimes at the end. The end element is usually

the one pluralized if it and other elements are so closely related as
to be considered a single word: *handfuls, housefuls, basketfuls.*
Just to confound the pluralizing of compound words, occasionally
more than one element is pluralized in the same word. Here
again, the best advice is: *Consult your dictionary.* The words
listed below illustrate the erratic principles stated in this paragraph:

attorney at law, attorneys at law
attorney general, attorneys general or attorney generals
brother-in-law, brothers-in-law
bystander, bystanders
commander in chief, commanders in chief
consul general, consuls general
father-in-law, fathers-in-law
hanger-on, hangers-on
major general, major generals
master sergeant, master sergeants
manservant, menservants
pailful, pailfuls
passer-by, passers-by
son-in-law, sons-in-law

Irregular Plurals

10. Some nouns have irregular plurals.

Surely you expected to read the statement above, sooner or later.
Here is a representative list of words with plurals that are irregular or plain nonsensical or which follow none of the principles
stated above. Try to master them by whatever device you have
found most useful:

alkali, alkalies   foot, feet
bison, bison   goose, geese
brother, brothers, brethren   louse, lice
child, children   madam, mesdames
deer, deer   man, men

moose, moose	sheep, sheep
mouse, mice	species, species
ox, oxen	swine, swine
photo, photos	tooth, teeth
series, series	woman, women

11. Pronouns and verbs have plural forms just as do nouns. It is doubtful, however, that misspelling of pronouns is due to their number. If you misspell *their*, a plural pronoun, you are probably confusing *their* and *there*, rather than having trouble with a plural. *We, they, our, us, them,* all plural pronouns, are easy to spell.

   The plurals of verbs are quite simple. Main verbs have the same form for both singular and plural except in the third person singular, present tense: he *sees*, he *moves*, he *thinks*, he *does*, he *goes*. That is, most verbs add an *s (es)* in the third person to form a singular. It's easy to remember this: most nouns and verbs form their plurals in directly opposite ways.

Nouns of Foreign Origin

12. Certain nouns of foreign origin retain the plural of the language from which they were borrowed. Some borrowed words have gradually assumed plurals with the usual English *s* or *es* endings. Finally, some words have more than one plural form.

To reduce confusion, here is a list of fairly common nouns to fix in your mind by whatever device works best for you:

addendum -da	appendix -dixes, -dices
alumna -nae	automaton -ta, -tons
alumnus -ni	axis -es
ameba -bae, -bas	bacillus -li
analysis -ses	basis -ses
apparatus -tus, -tuses	beau beaus, beaux

cactus -ti, -tuses
chateau -teaus, -teaux
cherub cherubs, cherubim
    (scriptural)
crisis -ses
criterion -ia
curriculum -lums, -la
datum -ta
diagnosis -ses
erratum -ta
focus -ci (scientific), -cuses
    (general)
formula -las, -lae
fungus -gi, -guses
gladiolus -luses, -li
hiatus -tuses, hiatus
hypothesis -ses
index indexes, indices
larva -vae
libretto -tos, -ti
locus l-ci
madame mesdames
matrix -trixes, -trices
medium -dia, -diums
memorandum -da, -dums
momentum -tums, -ta

monsieur messieurs
moratorium -iums, -ia
nebula -las, -lae
neurosis -ses
nucleus -clei, -cleuses
oasis -ses
opus opera, opuses
ovum -a
parenthesis -ses
psychosis -ses
radius radii, radiuses
rostrum -trums, -tra
species species
stadium -diums, -dia
stimulus -li
stratum -ta, -tums
syllabus -bi, -buses
synopsis -ses
synthesis -ses
tableau -bleaus, -bleaux
terminus -nuses, -ni
thesis -ses
trousseau -seaus, -seaux
vertebra -brae, -bras
vortex -tices, -texes
wagon-lits, wagons-lits

11

USE A DICTIONARY:

APOSTROPHES

An apostrophe is a mark of punctuation, not a letter, and yet when one is improperly added or omitted it causes you to misspell. The apostrophe has several uses, all with some influence on spelling:. to indicate the possessive case, to mark omission of letters, to indicate the plurals of letters and numbers. The use of an apostrophe influences both punctuation *and* spelling. Since this book deals only with spelling, we will concentrate on uses of the apostrophe which result in misspelling.

Indicating Possession

1. Use an apostrophe and *s* to form the possessive case of a noun (singular or plural) not ending in *s:*

   children, children's   horse, horse's
   doctor, doctor's   town, town's
           Children's shoes are often expensive.

2. Use only an apostrophe to form the possessive case of a plural noun ending in *s:*

   boys, boys'   students, students'
   ladies, ladies'   weeks, weeks'
           The boys' coats are in the closet.

3. Use an apostrophe alone or an apostrophe with *s* to form the possessive of singular nouns ending in *s:*

Robert Burns, Robert Burns' (or Burns's)
Charles, Charles' (or Charles's)

She liked Robert Burns' (or Burns's) poetry.
This is Charles' (or Charles's) hat.

4. In compound nouns add the apostrophe and *s* to the
   last element of the expression, the one nearest the object possessed:

   my son-in-law's boat   King Henry IV's funeral
   somebody else's ticket   the city manager's salary

Indicating Omission

5. Use an apostrophe to show that letters or figures have
   been omitted.

   aren't = are not   they're = they are
   don't = do not   wasn't = was not
   he's = he is   weren't = were not

   The Civil War was fought 1861–'65. (1861 to 1865)
   He left home in '59. (1959)

This use of the apostrophe is reflected in the most misspelled
short and simple word in the English language. *It's* means "it is"
and can never be correctly used for *its* in the possessive sense:
"When a dog wags *its* tail, that is a sign *it's* happy." Never write the
letters *i-t-s* without asking whether or not you mean "it is."

Forming Plurals

6. Use an apostrophe and *s* to indicate the plurals of figures, letters, and words considered as words.

   Small children cannot always make legible 5's.
   Uncrossed *t*'s look like *l*'s.
   He uses too many *and*'s and *but*'s in speaking.

7. Never use an apostrophe in forming the plural of nouns and the possessive case of personal relative pronouns.

The *Browns* (not *Brown's*) came to see us.

CORRECT	INCORRECT
ours	our's
ours	ours'
yours	your's
yours	yours'
his	his'
hers	her's
hers	hers'
its	it's
theirs	their's
theirs	theirs'
whose	who's

The apostrophe is essential in the correct spelling of numerous words and expressions. For each numbered part of the following sentences, choose a letter to indicate the preferred spelling.

1. I (*a.* do'nt; *b.* dont; *c.* don't) know
2. (*a.* whose; *b.* who's; *c.* whos') going
3. to win this (*a.* year; *b.* year's; *c.* years'; *d.* years) scholastic award.
4. We met the (*a.* Browns; *b.* Brown's; *c.* Browns') last night
5. at my (*a.* brother-in-law; *b.* brother's-in-law; *c.* brother-in-law's) house.
6. Among all the (*a.* children's; *b.* childrens; *c.* childrens') galoshes parked
7. in the hall, I hardly knew which were (*a.* hers; *b.* her's).
8. The common belief that the Japanese pronounce their (*a.* l's; *b.* ls'; *c.* ls)
9. to sound like the American r (*a.* isnt; *b.* isn't; *c.* is'nt) quite correct;

10. actually (*a.* its; *b.* it's; *c.* its') an intermediate sound not heard in English.

11. Remember that (*a.* anyone else; *b.* anyone's else; *c.* anyone else's; *d.* anyone else')

12. opinion has as good a chance of being right as (*a.* your; *b.* yours; *c.* your's).

13. The (*a.* Jones; *b.* Jones'; *c.* Joneses; *d.* Jones's) telephoned last night to say

14. that (*a.* they're; *b.* their; *c.* there) arriving on Tuesday.

15. It (*a.* can't; *b.* ca'nt; *c.* cant) have been much before

16. twelve (*a.* oclock; *b.* o'clock; *c.* o clock) that he came in.

17. For five (*a.* hour; *b.* hours; *c.* hour's; *d.* hours') work

18. (*a.* Jess; *b.* Jess'; *c.* Jesses; *d.* Jess's) pay was $18.60.

19. The (*a.* repairmen's; *b.* repairmens'; *c.* repairmen) demand for a raise in pay

20. was reasonable, but (*a.* its; *b.* it's) timing was unfortunate.

12

USE A DICTIONARY:

COMPOUND WORDS

The centuries-old tendency of the English language to combine words has created still another difficult problem for spellers. Even so, compound words have greatly increased the range and richness of the language and have provided many shortcuts and timesavers.

Now look at the paragraph that you have just read. Note that *centuries-old* is a compound written with a hyphen; that *shortcuts* and *timesavers* are compounds written as one word (no hyphen, no separation). Any one of these words written otherwise would be misspelled.

There are no rules or principles covering *all* combinations. Some few principles, easily learned, are discussed below, but for spelling the bulk of compound words you must use your dictionary whenever you are in doubt.

Principles of Word Joining

The general principle of word joining derives from actual usage. When two (or more) words first become associated with a single meaning, they are written separately. As they grow, through usage, to become more of a unit in thought and writing, they are usually hyphenated (spelled with a hyphen). Finally, they tend to be spelled as one word. This evolution may be seen in the following, the third word in each series now being the accepted form: *base ball, base-ball, baseball; rail road, rail-road, railroad*. This general principle, however, is not always in operation; many common expressions which one might think in the third stage are still in the first: *mother tongue, girl scout, in fact, high school.*

Here is another way to demonstrate how seemingly illogical is the spelling of many compound words: look up in your dictionary some of the words which have *red* as the first part of the compound. Dictionaries differ among themselves, but the one the author consulted shows these distinctions: *red cedar, red cent, red clover, Red Cross, red deer, red light, red man, red oak, red pepper, red rose,* and *red tape; red-blooded, red-headed, red-hot,* and *red-letter; redbud, redcap, redcoat, redhead, redwing,* and *redwood.*

The hyphenated *red* words above offer a clue. The hyphen is a device to separate and also a mark to unify, to join. As a mark of spelling, it both joins and separates two or more words used *as an adjective.* And yet it may or may not be called for in forming compound adjectives because of position in a given sentence. For example, hyphens are generally used between the parts of an adjective preceding the substantive (noun) which it modifies but may properly be omitted if the compound adjective follows. You may write "He saw the *red-hot* coil" and just as correctly write "The coil was *red hot.*" Since this is a book on spelling, not syntax, this illustration will have to serve as a warning and as a further plea for you to "look it up" whenever you are doubtful. But remember that dictionaries differ; they do not always indicate the distinction just made.

Finally, you should note that two or more words compounded may have a meaning quite different from that of the same two words not really joined:

Jim was a *battle-scarred* veteran.
The *battle scarred* the body and soul of Jim.
In this quarrel Sue served as a *go-between.*
The ball must *go between* the goal posts.

There is neither a shortcut nor an all-inclusive rule for spelling compound words. But perhaps it will be of some help to remember that the present-day tendency is to avoid the use of hyphens whenever possible.

Seven Classes of Compound Words

There are seven groups, or classes, of compound words with which the hyphen is used:

1. Two or more words modifying a substantive and used as a single adjective.

The hyphen is especially needed in combinations placed *before* the word modified. Examples of these combinations are:

   a. adjective, noun, or adverb + participle (+ noun)
      Bob is a *sad-looking* boy.
      Bell-shaped hats are in fashion again.
      He jumped from a *fast-moving* train.
   b. adjective + adjective (+ noun)
      Mary has *bluish-gray* eyes.
   c. adjective + noun (+ noun)
      He is a *first-rate* musician.
   d. noun + adjective (+ noun)
      There will be a *city-wide* search for the criminal.
   e. prefix + capitalized adjective (+ noun)
      We took a *trans-Atlantic ship* to England.

The following are other instances of the combinations mentioned above:

able-bodied	loose-tongued
above-mentioned	midnight-black
absent-minded	ocean-blue
Anglo-Saxon	rose-red
best-known	six-room
far-fetched	soft-spoken
good-natured	stiff-necked
Latin-American	ten-foot
light-haired	un-American
long-needed	wild-eyed

   2. Compound nouns.

Compound nouns consist of from two to as many as four parts.
Practically every part of speech can become a component of a
compound noun.

>   a. Two-part compound noun.
>   Coke is a *by-product* of coal. (preposition + noun)
>   b. Three-part compound noun.
>   My *brother-in-law* is a lawyer. (noun + preposition
>   + noun)
>   c. Four-part compound noun.
>   Harry is a *jack-of-all-trades.* (noun + preposition +
>   adjective + noun)

Other examples of compound nouns are the following:

court-martial	leveling-off
ex-president	looker-on
fellow-citizen	mother-in-law
forget-me-not	secretary-treasurer
go-between	son-in-law
great-grandson	tête-à-tête

>   3. Compound words with *half, quarter,* or *self* as the first
>   element.

half-and-half	self-conceit
half-asleep	self-control
half-truth	self-interest
quarter-final	self-made
quarter-hour	self-respect
quarter-share	self-sacrifice

>   4. Compound words made from a single capital letter and
>   a noun or participle:

A-flat	S-curve
F-sharp	T-shirt

5. "Improvised" compounds:

holier-than-thou   make-believe
know-it-all   never-say-die
long-to-be-remembered   never-to-be-forgotten

6. Compound numerals from twenty-one through ninety-nine:

thirty-three   sixty-seven
forty-six   eighty-five

7. The numerator and denominator of fractions:

four-fifths   three-quarters
one-half   two-thirds

If the hyphen already appears in either numerator or denominator it is omitted in writing the fraction:

twenty-one thirds   three ten-thousandths

General Cautions in Using the Hyphen

a. All the examples cited above were checked in a good desk dictionary. If your dictionary differs, don't hesitate to take its word.
b. Do not use a hyphen when two adjectives preceding a noun are independent:
    She wore a *faded yellow* hat.
c. Do not use a hyphen when an adverb modifies an adjective:
    She was a *highly trained* secretary.
d. Do not use a hyphen between double terms that denote a single office or rank:
    Major General Jones   *Executive Director* Adams
e. Omit the hyphen in writing a fraction that is not an adjective:
    He ate up *one half* of the pie.

f. Do not use a hyphen with reflexive pronouns:

     herself   *himself*   *yourselves*

g. Many compounds formerly spelled separately or with a hyphen are now written as single words:

     almighty   *inasmuch*   *namesake*

Once again, but finally, the only way to be sure about every compound word is to consult your dictionary.

Now apply what you have learned about compounds in the following exercise. In each of these phrases, decide whether the italicized expression should be written as one word, with hyphens, or as separate words. If you get stuck, consult your dictionary.

1. some *air minded* legislators
2. an important *air base*
3. excessive *rain fall*
4. a *base ball* game
5. in the *Far East*
6. a *battle hardened* veteran
7. the age of *twenty seven*
8. at *loose ends*
9. given a *rain check*
10. several *teen agers*
11. a *self satisfied* expression
12. a *holier than thou* attitude
13. in the *ante room*
14. a torn *book mark*
15. a broken *carpet sweeper*
16. in a *department store*
17. standing *flat footed*
18. got his *sheep skin*
19. *two way* road ahead
20. a sale of *re treads*
21. having only *self less* motives
22. a great *do it yourself* man
23. *un American* activities
24. an *anti climactic* ending
25. having been *re elected*
26. the *under developed* countries
27. a *well organized* conspiracy
28. a medieval *city state*
29. this *widely held* misconception
30. a sale of *pre empted* land
31. a row of *semi detached* houses
32. the fund was *over subscribed*
33. a *never to be forgotten* experience
34. an experience *never to be forgotten*
35. in the *living room*
36. a *pre dated* contract
37. a *poverty stricken* region
38. he was *well known* as an auctioneer
39. an attack of *home sickness*
40. a *hard hearted* landlord

13

USE A DICTIONARY:

CAPITALIZATION

Strictly speaking, a discussion of capital letters does not belong in a spelling book. One can argue with some reason that if a word contains all the right letters in the right places it is correctly spelled.

It is true that man has had to invent distinctions between capital letters and small letters and that these distinctions have varied from century to century and from author to author. At one time, for example, it was customary to capitalize all nouns, as it still is in writing German. Gradually, however, certain modern customs involving capital letters evolved. These customs aren't particularly logical. Perhaps because capitalization is as illogical as spelling and quite as much a matter of accident and convention it deserves discussion in this book.

The Conventions of Capital Letters

To misspell is to violate a convention; to use capital letters wrongly is to violate a convention. And breaking conventions, as all of us know, can cause us embarrassment, anguish, money, or all three. Many people firmly believe that mistakes in using capital and small letters are as serious as misspelling. Indeed, they feel that such mistakes *are* misspellings.

The applications of capitalization are so numerous, and so loaded with exceptions, that firm rules and principles cannot apply to every possible example. A few underlying principles may be helpful and are given below. The only sound principle for you to follow is *use a dictionary*.

Capitalizing First Words

1. Capitalize the first word of every sentence and the first word of every direct quotation.

   The engine needs repair.
   He asked, "Does the engine need repair?"

When only a part of a direct quotation is included within a sentence, it is usually not begun with a capital letter.

The reporter told me that the official said he felt "fine" but thought that he should "take it easy" for a few weeks.

Capitalizing Proper Nouns

2. Capitalize proper nouns. Proper nouns include:

   a. Names of people and titles used for specific persons: George Washington, Theodore Roosevelt, the President, the Senator, the Treasurer, the General, Mr. Chairman, Father, Mother.
   b. Names of countries, states, regions, localities, other geographic areas, and the like: United States, England, Illinois, the Far East, the Dust Bowl, the Midwest, the Solid South, the Rocky Mountains, the Sahara Desert, the Connecticut River, Lake Michigan.
   c. Names of streets: Michigan Boulevard, Fifth Avenue, Ross Street, Old Mill Road.
   d. Names of the Deity and personal pronouns referring to Him: God, Heavenly Father, Son of God, Jesus Christ, Saviour, His, Him, Thy, Thine.
   e. Names for the Bible and other sacred writings: Bible, the Scriptures, Book of Genesis, Revelation, Koran.

f. Names of religions and religious groups: Protestantism, Roman Catholicism, Presbyterian, Jesuit, Unitarian, Judaism, Shinto, Muslim, Islam.

g. Names of the days and the months (but *not* the seasons): Monday, Tuesday, etc.; January, February, etc.; summer, winter, autumn, fall, spring.

h. Names of schools, colleges, universities: Woodberry Forest School, Kentucky Military Institute, Davidson College, Cornell University.

i. Names of historic events, eras, and holidays: Revolutionary War, Christian Era, Middle Ages, Renaissance, the Fourth of July, Labor Day, Thanksgiving.

j. Names of races, organizations, and members of each: Indian, Negro, Malay, League of Women Voters, the Junior League, American Academy of Science, National League, San Francisco Giants, Big Ten Conference, an Elk, a Shriner, a Socialist.

k. Vivid personifications: Fate, Star of Fortune, Destiny, the power of Nature, the paths of Glory, the chronicles of Time, Duty's call.

l. Trade names: Bon Ami, Mr. Clean, Ry-Krisp, Wheaties, Anacin.

Note: If the reference is to any one of a class of persons or things rather than to a specific person or thing, do not capitalize the noun or adjective:

He is not a captain.
His name is Captain Draper.
I am going to a theater.
He is at the Bijou Theater.
He attended high school.
He attended Sumter High School.
In college he took history and biology.
In college he took History 12 and Biology 3.

Capitals in Poetry and in Titles

3. Capitalize the first word of every line of poetry:

I held it truth, with him who sings
To one clear harp in divers tones,
That men may rise on stepping-stones
Of their dead selves to higher things.
                                    —TENNYSON

4. Capitalize each important word in the title of a book, play, magazine, musical composition, etc.:

The Decline and Fall of the Roman Empire
You Can't Go Home Again
Romeo and Juliet
Atlantic Monthly
Madame Butterfly

The Careless Use of Capital Letters

5. Avoid unnecessary and careless use of capitals.

a. Do not carelessly make small (lower-case) letters so large that they resemble capitals (upper-case letters).

b. Do not capitalize names of points of the compass unless they refer to a specific section.

He lives in the West.
He walked west along the street.

c. Capitalize nouns such as *father* and *mother* if they are not preceded by a possessive.

Your father is a tall man.
I love Father very much.
My sister thinks I am noisy,
    but Grandpa says I am not.

Apply what you have learned about capitalization to situations presented in the following sentences. For each number in parentheses, decide whether the following word should begin with a capital or small letter.

The reporters next asked (1) general Coole for his opinion. The (2) general's only response was a terse (3) "no comment."

(1)_____; (2)_____; (3)_____.

At the first glow of dawn in the (4) east, the calm of the (5) equatorial jungle is shattered by an astonishing racket of bird cries and monkey calls; (6) even a person used to it is momentarily stunned.

(4)_____; (5)_____; (6)_____.

"If the (7) president is to retain the (8) southern vote," said Anderson, (9) "he will have to sacrifice some inner-city support in the (10) north."

(7)_____; (8)_____; (9)_____; (10)_____.

During the committee hearings (11) chairman Topper made frequent use of apt quotations from the (12) bible, which were probably more familiar to his (13) baptist constituents in (14) southern Mississippi than to the public at large.

(11)_____; (12)_____; (13)_____; (14)_____.

"I knew I could count on (15) mother's support," she said, (16) "but how could I break the news to my (17) father? (18) he's dead set against my leaving home."

(15)_____; (16)_____; (17)_____; (18)_____.

In recent years it has been customary for the (19) national (20) league to win the (21) all-star (22) game but to lose the (23) world (24) series, yet nothing is likely to shake the confidence of that (25) league's fans in its superiority.

(19)_____; (20)_____; (21)_____; (22)_____; (23)_____; (24)_____;
(25)_____.

The rather chilling scientific name for the (26) grizzly (27) bear, once found throughout the (28) rocky (29) mountain (30) range, is *Ursus horribilis*, although it is in fact less dangerous than the (31) polar (32) bear, which carries the relatively mild designation of (33) *thalarctos* (34) *maritimus*.

(26)_____; (27)_____; (28)_____; (29)_____; (30)_____; (31)_____;
(32)_____; (33)_____; (34)_____.

One of the little-noticed features of (35) homecoming (36) day was an illustrated lecture by (37) professor Folkes on archaeological finds in the (38) middle (39) east, of interest to students of both (40) history and the (41) fine (42) arts.

(35)_____; (36)_____; (37)_____; (38)_____; (39)_____; (40)_____; (41)_____; (42)_____.

Several characteristics of the repellent (43) utopia pictured in Aldous Huxley's novel *Brave* (44) *new World*, supposedly a projection into the twenty-fifth (45) century, are already appearing in today's (46) world.

(43)_____; (44)_____; (45)_____; (46)_____.

The teams of many (47) universities are known by their totem animals, such as the (48) badger, chosen by Wisconsin, and the (49) wolverine, by Michigan, but some other schools, such as Syracuse (50) university, maintain their athletic ferocity without the aid of feral symbols. In football games of recent years, perhaps by a decree of (51) nature, the (52) wolverines have usually overcome the (53) badgers.

(47)_____; (48)_____; (49)_____; (50)_____; (51)_____; (52)_____; (53)_____.

14

LEARN A FEW SIMPLE RULES
OF SPELLING

If you happen to study carefully a number of words which have similar characteristics, you can make some generalizations about their spelling. In fact, observers have been doing just this for more than a century with the result that nearly fifty spelling rules have been formulated.

Generalizations about the groupings of letters which form classes of words will definitely help some people to spell more correctly. Those with good visual or motor memories will not need them. Other people apparently have a psychological block against rules. But experience has shown that rules—or at least a few of the more basic ones—do help some people to spell correctly certain classes of words. Applying spelling rules is only one approach to correct spelling; it may be more or less helpful to you than the other methods of attack presented in this book.

The rules which follow, with their corollaries, are simple and easily learned. Mastering them may help you to eliminate a large number of recurring errors in fairly common words. If this approach works for you, then consult other books on spelling or the section on orthography (spelling according to standard usage) in *Webster's New Collegiate Dictionary* for additional rules. The six rules stated and illustrated below are those which the author's experience has shown to be most useful and to apply to the largest number of commonly misspelled words.

Before studying the rules which follow, you should understand a few basic principles about them.

First, it is doubtful that anyone ever improved his spelling merely by saying a rule over and over to himself. Words come first, rules second; you should apply a rule, not merely memorize and mouth it.

Second, there are exceptions to every rule. And since there are so many exceptions you will need to use an additional approach: improve your visual or motor memory; use some remembering trick; consult your dictionary.

Third, the corollary and the reverse of every spelling rule are as important as the rule itself. For example, in the first rule given below, you are shown when not to use *i* before *e*, but the reverse of this pattern is fully as important and must be kept in mind and applied. Learning only part of a rule is about as silly and timewasting as looking up a word in a dictionary and learning only one meaning of it, or only its spelling.

The *EI–IE* Rule

One of the most frequent causes of misspelling is not knowing whether to write *ei* or *ie* in literally scores of everyday words. In fact, about one thousand fairly common words contain *ei* or *ie*. It helps to know that *ie* occurs in twice as many words as *ei*, but the problem is not thereby solved.

The basic rule may be stated in one of the best-known pieces of doggerel ever written:

> Write *i* before *e*
> Except after *c*
> Or when sounded like *a*
> As in *neighbor* and *weigh*.

This rule, or principle, applies only when the pronunciation of *ie* or *ei* is a long *e* (as in *he*) or the sound of the *a* in *fade*.

Here's another way to summarize the rule and its reverse:
   When the sound is long *e* (as in *piece*)
      put *i* before *e* except after *c*.
   When the sound is not long *e* (as it is not in *weigh*)
      put *e* before *i*.

Still another way to state this principle is this: When the *e* sound is long, *e* comes first after *c* but *i* comes first after all other consonants:

ceiling	deceit	receipt
conceit	deceitful	receive
conceited	deceive	
conceive	perceive	

achieve	apiece	believe
aggrieve	belief	besiege
bier	grieve	reprieve
brief	handkerchief	retrieve
cashier	hygiene	shield
chandelier	mischief	shriek
chief	piece	siege
field	pier	thief
fiend	pierce	wield
frontier	priest	wiener
grief	relieve	yield

This much of the rule is fairly simple: usually you write *ie*, except after the letter *c*, when you write *ei*—provided the sound is long *e*. The last two lines of the doggerel refer to words in which *ei* or *ie* sounds like *a*. Fortunately, only a few everyday words fall in this group, among them:

beige	heir	surveillance
chow mein	neigh	veil
deign	neighbor	vein
eight	reign	weigh
feint	rein	weight
freight	skein	
heinous	sleigh	

A few words are either exceptions to this basic *ei-ie* rule or are not fully covered by the four lines of doggerel. The best advice is to learn the following words by some method other than trying to apply the rule, which doesn't work here:

caffeine	height	seize
codeine	hierarchy	seizure
either	leisure	sheik
Fahrenheit	neither	sleight
fiery	protein	stein
financier	Reid (proper name)	weird

Summary

1. Use *ie* generally when sounded as long *e* (he).
2. Use *ei* after *c* when sounded as *e* (he).
3. Use *ei* when sounded as *a* (*eight*).
4. Watch out for exceptions.

The Final Y Rule

Forming the plural of nouns ending in *y* has already been discussed on page 112. But the rule applies also to words other than nouns and their plurals. The basic principle is this:

a. Words ending in *y* preceded by a consonant usually change *y* to *i* before any suffix except one beginning with *i*:

angry, angrily
beauty, beautiful
busy, busily, business
carry, carries, carrying
dignify, dignified, dignifying
easy, easier, easily
empty, emptier, emptiness
happy, happier, happiness
lovely, lovelier, loveliness
lucky, luckier, luckily
marry, married, marriage
merry, merrier, merrily, merriment
pity, pitiful, pitying
pretty, prettier, prettiness
study, studied, studious
try, tried, trying

b. Words ending in *y* preceded by a vowel do not change *y* to *i* before suffixes or other endings:

annoy, annoyed, annoyance   employ, employer
betray, betrayal   stay, stayed, staying

To the two parts of this "final *y*" rule there are so many exceptions that some experts feel the rule is not helpful. However, the exceptions among commonly used words are not numerous and can easily be mastered by some other approach suggested in this book. Here are some everyday words which follow neither part of the "final *y*" principle:

baby, babyhood   pay, paid
busy, busyness (state   say, said
  of being busy)   shy, shyly, shyness
day, daily   slay, slain
lady, ladyship   wry, wryly, wryness
lay, laid

The Final *E* Rule

Hundreds of everyday English words end in *e*, and hundreds and hundreds more consist of such words plus suffixes: *hope, hoping; come, coming; safe, safety*, etc. In our pronunciation nearly all *e*'s at the end of words are silent (not pronounced): *advice, give, live*, etc. Actually, the function of a final silent *e* is to make the vowel of the syllable long: *rate* but *rat; mete* but *met; bite* but *bit; note* but *not*, etc.

With those facts in mind we can now proceed to a rule which covers more words than any other spelling rule, many of them common words frequently misspelled. Here it is:

Final silent *e* is usually dropped before a suffix beginning with a vowel but is retained before a suffix beginning with a consonant.

advise, advising   believe, believing, believable
amuse, amusing, amusement   bite, biting
argue, arguing   care, careful, careless
arrive, arrival   come, coming
awe, awesome   desire, desirable
bare, barely, bareness   dine, dining

excite, exciting, excitement
extreme, extremely
hate, hateful
hope, hoping, hopeless
ice, icy
judge, judging
like, likable
live, livable

love, lovable
move, movable, movement
owe, owing
purchase, purchasing
safe, safely, safety
sincere, sincerely
sure, surely, surety
use, usable, useless

This basic rule is clear enough, but it does not cover all words ending in silent *e*. Here are some additions and exceptions to the general principle:

a. Silent *e* is retained when *ing* is added to certain words, largely to prevent them from being confused with other words:

   dye, dyeing to contrast with *die, dying*
   singe, singeing to contrast with *sing, singing*
   swinge, swingeing to contrast with *swing, swinging*
   tinge, tingeing to contrast with *ting, tinging*

b. Silent *e* is retained in still other words before a suffix beginning with a vowel. Sometimes this is done for the sake of pronunciation, sometimes for no logical reason at all:

   acre, acreage   line, lineage
   cage, cagey   mile, mileage
   here, herein   shoe, shoeing
   hoe, hoeing   there, therein

c. Silent *e* is dropped before a suffix beginning with a consonant in certain common words such as:

   abridge, abridgment   due, duly
   acknowledge, ac-   incredible, incredibly
      knowledgment   judge, judgment
   argue, argument   nine, ninth
   awe, awful   nurse, nursling
   double, doubly   possible, possibly

probable, probably   whole, wholly
true, truly   wise, wisdom
twelve, twelfth

d. Silent *e* is retained in words ending in *ce* or *ge* even
   when suffixes beginning with vowels (*-able* and *-ous*)
   are added. This is done for the sake of pronunciation: to
   prevent giving a hard sound (*k* or hard *g*) to the *c* or *g*:

marriage, marriageable   advantage, advantageous
notice, noticeable   courage, courageous
service, serviceable   outrage, outrageous

e. A few words ending in *ie* in which the *e* is silent change
   ie to *y* before adding *ing*. Presumably this change occurs to prevent two *i*'s from coming together:

die, dying   tie, tying (or tieing)
lie, lying   vie, vying

The Inserted *K* Rule

The letter *k* is usually added to words ending in *c* before a suffix
beginning with *e*, *i*, or *y*. This is done in order to prevent mispronunciation: note the different pronunciations, for example, of
picnicking and *icing*. Only a few common words are involved in
this rule, but they are frequently misspelled:

colic, colicky   picnic, picnicked, picnicker
frolic, frolicked, frolicking   politic, politicking
mimic, mimicked, mimicking   shellac, shellacked, shellacking
panic, panicky   traffic, trafficked, trafficking

This rule must be applied carefully. Note, for example, the words
frolicsome and *mimicry*. Without adding a *k*, each *c* remains hard.

The Final Consonant Rule

The rule for doubling final consonants is somewhat complicated,
but mastering it and its parts will prevent many common misspellings. Despite its complexity, it is one of the most useful rules
for spelling.

a. Words of one syllable and those of more than one accented on the last syllable, when ending in a single consonant (except *x*) preceded by a single vowel, double the consonant before a suffix beginning with a vowel.

This rule is fairly detailed, but it will repay careful study. It is especially helpful in forming the past tense, past participle, and present participle of many frequently used verbs. It is also helpful in forming the comparative and superlative degrees of adjectives. Here is a list of only a few of the thousands of words to which this principle applies:

> acquit, acquitted, acquitting, acquittal
> admit, admitted, admitting, admittance
> begin, beginning, beginner
> clan, clannish
> control, controlled, controller
> drop, dropped, dropping
> equip, equipped, equipping
> forget, forgetting, forgettable, unforgettable
> man, mannish
> occur, occurred, occurring, occurrence
> overlap, overlapped, overlapping
> plan, planned, planning
> prefer, preferred, preferring
> red, redder, reddest, redden
> refer, referred, referring
> run, running, runner
> swim, swimming, swimmer
> tax, taxes
> tin, tinny

b. If the accent is shifted to an earlier syllable when the ending is added, do not double the final consonant:

> confer, conferring, but conference
> defer, deferring, but deference
> infer, inferring, but inference
> prefer, preferring, but preference

c. Cautions and exceptions:

1) Derivatives from basic words that change pronunciation from a long to short vowel follow the doubling rule:

   bite, biting, but bitten
   inflame, inflamed, but inflammable
   write, writing, but written

2) Words ending in a final consonant preceded by *two* vowels do not double the final consonant:

   appear, appeared, appearing, appearance
   need, needed, needing, needy
   train, trained, training, trainee

3) Words ending in *two* consonants do not double the final consonant:

   bend, bending (not bendding)
   insist, insisted (not insistted)
   turn, turned (not turnned)

4) Words not accented on the final syllable do not ordinarily double the final consonant:

   benefit, benefited (but fit, fitted)
   happen, happened, happening
   murmur, murmured, murmuring

   A helpful word in fixing this principle in your mind is *combat*. It may be pronounced with the accent on either syllable, but note the spelling:

   | com bat′ | combatted | combatting |
   | com′bat | combated | combating |

5) Like all spelling rules, this one for doubling has many exceptions or apparent exceptions. Rather than try to apply the rule slavishly, you would gain by learning the following through some other approach suggested in this book:

cancellation	gaseous	overstepping
chagrined	handicapped	questionnaire
chancellor	humbugged	tranquillity
crystallize	legionnaire	transferable
excellence	metallurgy	transference
excellent	outfitter	zigzagged

The "One Plus One" Rule

When a prefix ends in the same letter with which the main part of the word begins, be sure that both letters are included.

When the main part of a word ends in the same letter with which a suffix begins, be sure that both letters are included.

When two words are combined, the first ending with the same letter with which the second begins, be sure that both letters are included.

Some spelling difficulties caused by prefixes and suffixes have been discussed in Chapters 8 and 9. The rule just stated in three parts is both supplementary and complementary to that discussion. It will take care of a larger number of often misspelled words such as:

accidentally	glowworm	really
bathhouse	illiterate	roommate
bookkeeping	interrelation	soulless
brownness	irresponsible	suddenness
cleanness	meanness	transshipment
coolly	misspelling	underrate
cruelly	occasionally	unnecessary
dissatisfied	overrated	unneeded
dissimilar	override	unnoticed
drunkenness	overrun	withholding

The only important exception to this rule is *eighteen* which, of course, is not spelled *eighteen*. Also, keep in mind that the same three consonants are never written solidly together: *cross-stitch*, not *crossstitch*; *still-life*, not *stilllife*. See the discussion of the hyphen (compound words) on pages 121–127.

15

SPELL CAREFULLY

This is a short chapter, but its brevity bears no relationship to its importance in spelling correctly. Actually, this chapter discusses the cause of at least half of the spelling mistakes made; for this reason, it is probably the most important chapter in this book.

When writing, you concentrate on what you are trying to say and not on such matters as grammar, punctuation, and spelling. This concentration is both proper and understandable. But in your absorption you are quite likely to make errors of various sorts, including some in spelling, which result from haste or carelessness, not ignorance. When you discover a mistake of this kind, or it is pointed out to you, you may reply "Oh, I know better. I just wasn't watching," or "thinking" or "being careful," or whatever excuse you choose to make.

The word processor has changed the method of discovering spelling mistakes for those writers who use such a device. It enables the writer automatically to check the spelling of an individual word or the words in a marked block of text. When words are in doubt, possible corrections are suggested. Advanced word processing systems can correct misspellings automatically the next time they appear.

Carelessness and Haste

Unfortunately, a mistake in spelling is a mistake until corrected. Your reader will not know, or care, what caused it. The office manager who received a letter from one of his staff recently inducted into the U.S. Army was delighted to hear from him, but was more annoyed than puzzled to read: "It was the *frist* time we had to march ten miles and I nearly *collasped*." Certainly the young soldier knew better; he intended to write *first* and *collapsed* but, through haste, carelessness, or failure to proofread, the mistakes went through.

Isn't it fair to suggest that since so many English words really are difficult to spell, we should be careful with those we actually know? And yet it is the simple, easy words which nearly everyone *can* spell that cause over half the errors commonly made. Listed below are twenty words which the author has repeatedly found misspelled in letters, reports, and student papers. They are so easy that you are likely to look at them scornfully and say, "I would never misspell any one of them." The fact is that you probably do misspell some of these words, on occasion, or other words just as simple:

all right, *not* alright	piano, *not* panio
a lot, *not* alot	radio, *not* raido
Britain, *not* Britian	religion, *not* regilion
curl, *not* crul	research, *not* reaserch
doesn't, *not* does'nt	surprise, *not* supprise
forty, *not* fourty	third, *not* thrid
high school, *not* highschool	thirty, *not* thrity
in fact, *not* infact	thoroughly, *not* throughly
in spite, *not* inspite	whether, *not* wheather
ninety, *not* ninty	wouldn't, *not* would'nt

Errors of this sort are easy to make. Our pen or pencil slips; a finger hits the wrong key; our minds wander. Even excellent spellers often repeatedly make such silly mistakes. What's the remedy?

Proofreading

Well, merely glancing over or even rereading what you've written is not likely to uncover all such errors. When we read we usually see only the outlines, or shells, of words. Only poor readers need to see individual letters as such; most of us comprehend words and even groups of words at a glance. As our eyes move along a line we neither see nor recognize individual letters and this, of course, is as it should be.

But have you ever noticed how much easier it is for you to detect spelling errors in someone else's writing than in your own? This may be because we are looking for mistakes. Or it may be that we look more carefully at the writing of someone else than at our own because we are unfamiliar with it, are not previously aware of context, and have to pay closer attention in order to comprehend.

Whatever the reason for closer scrutiny, we narrow the range of our vision and thereby pick up mistakes hitherto unnoticed. In short, we detect careless errors in spelling not by reading but by *proofreading*.

It is indeed naïve for any of us to think that we can write rapidly without misspelling some words, even though we are good spellers. Only careful proofreading will uncover spelling errors in our own writing or, indeed, in anyone else's.

This kind of reading requires that we see words and phrases not as such but that we actually see every letter they contain. When each letter stands out distinctly, it is simple to detect errors in spelling.

Vision Spread

This triangle will show you how wide your vision (your sight spread) is. Look at the top of the triangle and then down. How far down can you go and still identify each letter in each line with a *single* glance? Your central vision is as wide as the line above the one where you cannot identify each letter *without moving your eyes at all:*

a

a r

a r d

a r d c

a r d c f

a r d c f g

a r d c f g x

a r d c f g x y

a r d c f g x y z

a r d c f g x y z p

a r d c f g x y z p w

People differ in their range of vision as they do in nearly everything else. But most people have difficulty in identifying more than six letters at a single glance. Some have a span of vision embracing only three or four letters. Whatever your span, you should not try to exceed it when you are carefully checking for spelling errors. If you do, you are reading—perhaps with excellent understanding—but you are not *proofreading*. And only proofreading will enable you to eliminate spelling errors due not to ignorance or stupidity but to carelessness.

Here is a list of forty frequently misspelled words. Some are spelled correctly here; some are not. In which of them can you identify each letter at a single glance? Which require you to move your eyes even if only slightly?

1. acquaint	15. decide	29. preferable
2. against	16. extremely	30. primative
3. all right	17. field	31. process
4. amount	18. finishing	32. pursue
5. apear	19. likelyhood	33. recomendation
6. arise	20. lonely	34. representative
7. around	21. mere	35. restaurant
8. basas	22. noblity	36. sandwitch
9. before	23. noticeable	37. siege
10. begining	24. occupying	38. twelfth
11. careless	25. opportunity	39. unmanageable
12. clothes	26. optomistic	40. yield
13. comming	27. pamplet	
14. considerable	28. perseverance	

Eleven of these words are misspelled. Did your proofreading catch them all? Check your findings: the following contain errors—5, 8, 10, 13, 19, 22, 26, 27, 30, 33, 36.

Keep in mind that at least 50 percent of all errors come from omitting letters or transposing or adding them, writing two words as one or vice versa, and other similar acts of carelessness. Check and recheck, read and reread your writing until you have eliminated at least all the careless mistakes which everyone makes. There will still be errors enough of other kinds to keep you humble or angry.

Find out how well you can proofread. In the following paragraphs fifty words are misspelled. List these words on a sheet of paper by giving correct spellings of the incorrect words. To help you get started, here are the incorrect spellings in the first paragraph: *registeration, recieve, writting, approximatly,* and *convient.* Keep proofreading until you locate exactly fifty words. If a word is spelled incorrectly more than once, list it only once.

1.

After I had been admitted to Atwood University and had completed my registeration, I was very much surprised to recieve a letter from my grandfather. Now, Grandfather was never very much of a man for writting letters, but approximatly every week or so his communications continued to arrive. I am sure that at times it was not convient for him to write (he as much as said so frequently), but he had the urge, so he said, to tell me of his own experiences at Atwood.

2.

Grandfather early wrote about my making friends. He had made the aquaintance, he said, of many people during his first weeks at Atwood, from whom he chose a few intimates. These people he had met in the classroom, at some of the fraternities, in the Union, in resturants, and on the atheletic field. He treated every one in a courtious manner and never cracked jokes at their expense; so doing, he had learned, was a sure way to forfiet their respect.

3.

One of Grandfather's closest associates was Bill Jones, whom he had met at one of the dormatories. Bill was a very tempermental person, but he had a genius for getting along with people, and Grandfather benefited greatly from his comradship. About the middle of the first semester they became roomates.

4.

From Bill Jones Grandfather learned much about the art of studying. Up to the time of their rooming togeather, Grandfather was much dissatisfied with his scholastic record, and even though he tried to learn to study, he sometimes was so poorly prepared, usually in mathmatics and English, that he was almost too embarassed to go to class. Bill made a begining of his work on Grandfather's scholarship by giving him simple explainations of his more difficult assignments, but he was more interested in teaching the methods and dicipline of study. Once Grandfather had mastered these, the maintainance of better marks became an easy task.

5.

One of Bill's secrets was concentration; if you divide your attention, you get nowhere. Another was not postponing getting to work. Grandfather admitted, for example, that the night before one test, he spent the evening playing pool at the Union. He had alloted two hours for his review, but the evening just seemed to dissappear, and when Grandfather got to his room, he was too tired to worry about his lack of knowlege, and went immediatly to bed. He was not much mistified when he failed the test, and he even thought of quiting school. But about that time he met Bill and aquired valuble study habits. No longer was he an irresponsable student, handicaped by a lack of study method. Study was now his first neccessary task. When the next test came, he was so good that he could spot an independant clause a paragraph away; and by the time of the punctuation test, he had mastered the comma, had good control of the semicoln, and was even using recklessly but correctly quite a number of ap-postrophes.

6.

In high school Grandfather had been a notorously poor speller. The adolescent love notes that Grandfather wrote to the girl accross the aisle contained so many wrongly spelled words that the young lady broke off the correspondance. Love couldn't erradicate Grandfather's spelling disease, and after this disasterous adventure he swore that he would overcome his trouble; but he didn't. It was method, not love, that Grandfather needed, and Bill Jones supplied the answer. Grandfather still spelled a word wrong occassionally, but he became so persistent in his study of the words spelled by rule, the tricky words, and the words spelled according to sylable that when he took the spelling test for the first time, he had only one mispelled word.

7.

I could go on and on telling of the refferences to college life made in Grandfather's letters, and of the many occurences of which he wrote. But I don't want to be accused of wordyness, and, anyway, I've given you a general idea of the content of these letters.

8.

Long before the end of the year I became conscious of the fact that Grandfather was trying to decieve me in a polite way; he was really giving me advice by means of his letters, but whenever I accused him of this fact, he swore to his innocense and vowed that his only object was to entertain me and, perhaps, keep me from becoming homesick. I never did quite beleive him.

16

USE MEMORY DEVICES

Suppose that someone suddenly asks you, "How many days in March?" You may be able to answer instantly, but if you are like most of us you will come up with the answer, "thirty-one," only after you have run through your head the familiar lines beginning, "Thirty days hath September . . ." If so, what you have done is to use a device to aid memory.

One special kind of memory device has the rather imposing name of *mnemonics*. The word is pronounced *nee*-MON-*iks* and comes from a Greek word meaning "to remember." (Mnemosyne was the goddess of memory in Greek mythology.) A mnemonic is a special aid to memory, a memory trick based on what psychologists refer to as "association of ideas," remembering something by associating it with something else. You may have been using mnemonics most of your life. The term applies to a very basic characteristic of the human mind.

For example, the author's physician used to confuse his home, office, and hospital telephone numbers. He could remember the exchanges all right, but frequently mixed up the three sets of four numbers which followed, sometimes with unfortunate results. Now he has no difficulty: his home number he associates with eating and the numbers 1-8-4-7 leap to mind as part of "Rogers 1847 Silverware." His office number represents the place where he *battles* the daily grind and he thinks of the date of the Battle of Hastings, "1066." The hospital is a place where many find peace and relief from pain; the doctor associates this idea with "1945," the end of World War II. His set of mnemonics has licked the problem for him. When the telephone company assigns different numbers, he will probably invent other memory aids. In our own lives each of us quite likely uses many similar associations of ideas, however different they may be in details from those of the physician just mentioned.

Mnemonics as a Spelling Aid

Mnemonics *can* be used to improve spelling. The system will help some more than others and may not help some people at all. The entire system of association of ideas has been criticized because, of course, you can place a greater burden on your mind with elaborate mnemonics than is involved in the original item to be remembered. In addition, a memory aid that works for you may be useless to me, and vice versa. But a set of mental associations has proved useful to some people for spelling certain words, and a system of mnemonics is one legitimate approach to better spelling. The system is the main trade trick of memory experts for whom it works with astounding results.

As other chapters in this book try to show, the spelling of most words can be learned by improving visual or motor images and by spelling rules. But for each of us there probably is a small number of words the spelling of which is always troublesome. They fit no pattern; their spelling makes little or no sense. Learning them is a matter of sheer memory. For such words, an association of ideas may help. At least it will be more profitable than mouthing the hard words repeatedly or writing them over and over until they seem formless or grotesque.

Any mnemonic is a sort of crutch, something we use until we can automatically spell a given word without even thinking. But so is a rule a crutch, and, in a different sense, a dictionary is, too. In time, we can throw away our spelling crutches except on rare occasions; until then we can use them to avoid staggering and falling.

A mnemonic will be most helpful when you contrive it from some happening, or base it upon some person, meaningful in your life. That is, you must invent, or use, only mnemonics that have a *personal* association of ideas. Some of the mnemonics suggested below will help you; others will seem meaningless or downright silly. Some words which trouble you will not even be covered. You can then try devising mnemonics of your own for your particular spelling demons.

As was suggested in Chapter 5, a clue about the etymology or origin of a word will sometimes provide a mnemonic. Sometimes exaggerated pronunciation will form the association, the bond of relationship between word and spelling. Occasionally, breaking the word into parts will help. Sometimes a play on words will give a useful memory device. As you read the mnemonics below, you will note these and various other methods used in manufacturing them. On occasion, you will see that more than one method is used to phrase a mnemonic for the same word. Adapt for your use the most helpful one.

Memory Clues to Selected Troublesome Words

If none of these mnemonics proves helpful, you will at least have suggestions for "rolling your own." If another approach to correct spelling better suits your learning abilities, then skip what follows. At any rate, these memory clues have helped some people to spell correctly the words listed:

all right—Two words. Associate with **all correct** or **all wrong.**

anoint—Use **an oil** to **anoint** him (each **n** appears alone).

argument—I lost an **e** in that **argument.**

balloon—Remember the **ball** in **balloon.**

battalion—This comes from **battle;** it has the same double **t** and single **l.**

believe—You can't believe a **lie.**

business—Business is no **sin.**

calendar—The **D.A.R.** will meet soon.

capitol—A capit**ol** has a d**o**me (associate **o**).

cemetery—1. There is **ease** (**e**'s) in the cemetery.
             2. A place we get to with **ease** (**e**'s).

compliment—A compliment is what **I** like to get.

conscience—con + science.

corps—Don't kill a live body of men with an **e** (corpse).

definite—Definite comes from **finite.**

dependable—An **able** worker is dependable.

descendant—A descendant has an ancestor.

desert—The Sahara (one **s**).

dessert—Strawberry sundae (two **s**'s).

dilemma—In a dilemma was **Emma.**

disappoint—dis + appoint.

dormitory—The French word for sleep is **dormir.**

ecstasy—There is no **x** in ecstasy.

embarrassed—1. Double **r**, double **s**, double trouble.

2. **R**obert and **R**ose were **sh**op **st**ewards.

February—February makes one say "**Br!**"

genealogy—**Al** is interested in genealogy.

grammar—1. Accent the trouble spot: grammar.

2. Don't **mar** your writing with bad grammar.

3. Write **g—r—a—m:** then start back: **m—a—r.**

hear—I hear with my **ear.**

indispensable—1. **Able** people are indispensable.

2. This word refers to a thing one is not **able** to **dispense** with.

3. **Sable** is indispensable to some women.

infinite—Infinite comes from **finite.**

inoculate—Inoculate means to **inject.**

irresistible—1. **I** am irresistible to the opposite sex.

2. Lipstick is irresistible.

laboratory—People **labor** in a laboratory.

literature—It was an **era** of good literature.

medicine—Associated with **medicinal.**

occasion—1. An occasion occurs.

2. Don't be an **ass** on this occasion (one **s**).

occurrence—An occurrence may be a **current** event.

outrageous—The outrageous idea put me in a **rage.**

parallel—**All** lines are parallel.

piece—Have a piece of **pie.**

potatoes—Potatoes have eyes and **toes.**

preparation—1. From the base word **prepare**.
     2. This comes from *prae* + *parare* (to make ready).

principal—A principal rule is a main rule.

principle—A principle is just a ru**le**.

privilege—Some special privi**le**ges are **vile**.

professor—The abbreviation is **prof** (one **f**).

pronunciation—The **nun** knew pro**nun**ciation.

pursuit—A pickpocket took my **purse**.

recommend—re + commend.

relative—**Relative** comes from **relate**.

repetition—Associate with "**repeat**."

resistance—Increase resis**tan**ce with **tan**.

ridiculous—Associate with **ridicule**.

seize—Seize him by the **ear** (**e** before **i**).

separate—1. Separate means "apart."
    2. Accent the trouble spot: separate.
    3. There is a **rat** in sepa**rat**e.

sergeant—Think of **serge** + **ant**.

siege—An army sits before a city (**i** before **e**).

significant—"Sign if I cant" (can't).

stationary—This word means "standing."

stationery—This is used for writing le**tters**.

superintendent—A superintend**ent** collects **rent**.

supersede—1. Both first and last syllables begin with **s**.
     2. The word comes from Latin *sedeo*, "to sit."

surprise—That was **surely** a **surprise**.

temperature—She lost her **temper at** the heat.

together—to + get + her.

tragedy—1. Every **age** has its trage**dy**.
    2. Old **age** may be a trage**dy**.

tranquillity—Associate with **quill** (pens used in olden days).

vaccine—Vaccine is measured in **c**ubic **c**entimeters (**cc**'s).

villain—The **villa**in likes his **villa in** the country.

Wednesday—This word means "Woden's day."

17

LISTING MISSPELLED
WORDS

This chapter, the one with which many books on spelling begin, discusses an important phase of spelling study. It has been placed later for several reasons.

One reason is that learning to spell is an individual, highly personal matter. As we have discovered, a single approach to correct spelling will work for one person and not for another. Also, the words whose spelling gives you trouble may not be the words which bother me or any of your friends and acquaintances. Perhaps it would be more precise to say that, although certain words cause trouble for a majority of people, any list of commonly misspelled words will contain some that give you no difficulty and omit others that do. The very best list of words for you to study is the one you prepare yourself to meet your own needs and shortcomings.

The Value of Spelling Lists

There's a lot of waste in any spelling list, including the list of 860 words which follows. It is simple to prepare a list of "spelling demons" and assert that these are the "most frequently misspelled" words in the language. In a sense, this statement would be correct, but it fails to recognize that, although these words are likely to be misspelled when used, they aren't used very often. Learning to spell a long list of difficult words is about as vain as trying to swallow a dictionary or an encyclopedia. You use a dictionary when you need to tap its resources, just as you turn a faucet to get water from a reservoir. You consult a list of misspelled words only when you have a definite need.

Another reason for deferring this chapter toward the end is that by now you should have a sound basis for considering its contents. It doesn't help to try to memorize a list of miscellaneous words. But with what you have learned about various attacks on the spelling problem you can now *study* words in a list and *apply* to them principles you have learned.

Furthermore, you will be able to ignore words which you can already spell "without thinking" and will be alert to add words which give you trouble but which don't appear.

Once again, this chapter should serve primarily to start you on a list of your personal spelling demons. These words will be ones you need to learn to spell because you use them. And they may be simple or difficult; short or long; everyday words or ones which, although rare to others, are a part of your working vocabulary. The only sound basis for any list of misspelled words is its *use* value.

Regardless of whether we are housewives, businessmen, clerks, truckdrivers, or physicians, we all use certain basic words many scores of times more often than any others in the language. Any spelling list should start with them, but, fortunately, they are never (or hardly ever) misspelled by anyone who can write at all. The most frequently used words in the English language are *and, the, to, you, your, in, for, of, we, is, I*, and *its*. These give no trouble except for some occasional confusion between *your* and *you're* and *its* and *it's*.

Once past this basic list, however, selecting frequently used words becomes more difficult. *Table* is an everyday word, but a baker might use *bread* and a physician might use *temperature* more often. It is reassuring to know, however, that it is neither the most simple and common words nor the ones primarily used in a trade, profession, or industry that provide major spelling difficulty. The words in between are the troublemakers. And here we do have some authoritative studies of frequency word use and frequency misspellings. The short list which follows is based upon one of these major studies.

The Twenty Most Often Misspelled Words

Of the five hundred words occurring most frequently in our speech and writing only twenty ever cause anyone except very poor spellers any trouble whatever. Probably few, if any, of them bother you. Here is the list:

across	dollar	possible	suppose
almost	don't	quite	their
believe	friend	receive	through
brought	government	should	whether
business	laugh	supply	your

Keep in mind that these twenty words, along with 480 even more easily spelled ones, are certain to appear in your speech and writing many times as often as all other words in the language. The best approach of all to correct spelling is to *master* the simple, everyday words that you use over and over. Doing so will solve the greater part of your spelling problem.

According to another authoritative estimate, previously quoted, a basic list of only one thousand words appears in 90 percent of all writing. Most of the thousand which involve spelling problems are included in the long list which follows. About 75 percent of the words which follow are among the words most often misspelled regardless of frequency use. The other 25 percent consist of words which the author has found repeatedly misspelled in business offices, in manuscripts submitted for magazine or book publication, and in college classrooms.

As suggested, many of the words you will have already mastered; you must supplement the list in accordance with your own needs. But remember to go slowly. Don't try to memorize the list. Thoroughly mastering five words a day is more productive than superficially learning one hundred.

And as you start studying the list of words, apply one or more of the varied approaches suggested in previous chapters. Examining these words without following one or several of the planned attacks discussed in this book will merely waste your time and result in further and prolonged frustration.

Consult your dictionary frequently. You must know the meaning of each of the words you are studying; otherwise, in your own writing you may correctly spell a perfectly good word but one which does not have the meaning you intended. Also, to keep this list within reasonable limits, not all forms of every word are shown; therefore, use your dictionary or one of the other approaches developed in previous chapters as a guide to word-building.

List of 860 Words Often Misspelled*

1. absence
2. absolutely
3. academic
4. accept
5. access
6. accessible
7. accident
   (accidentally)
8. accommodate
   (accommodations)
9. accompanying
10. accomplishment
11. according
12. accumulation
13. accurate
14. accuse
15. accustomed
16. ache
17. achievement
18. acknowledge
    (acknowledgment)
19. acquaint (acquaintance)

* The list given has been checked against some of the major studies of frequency word use and frequency misspelling of the last forty years, as follows:

William Niclaus Andersen, "Determination of a Spelling Vocabulary Based upon Written Correspondence," *University of Iowa Studies in Education*, II, No. 1 (1917).

Alfred Farrell, "Spelling as a College Subject," *Journal of Education*, CXXII (January 1939), 20, 21.

Arthur I. Gates, *Spelling Difficulties in 3876 Words* (New York: Bureau of Publications, Teachers College, Columbia University, 1937).

John G. Gilmartin, *Gilmartin's Word Study*, rev. ed. (New York: Prentice-Hall, 1936).

Harry V. Masters, "A Study of Spelling Errors," *University of Iowa Studies in Education*, IV, No. 4 (1927–1929).

Thomas Clark Pollock, "Spelling Report," *College English*, XVI (November 1954), 102–109.

Edward L. Thorndike and Irving Lorge, *The Teacher's Word Book of 30,000 Words* (New York: Bureau of Publications, Teachers College, Columbia University, 1944).

20. across
21. activities
22. actual (actually)
23. address
24. adequate
25. adjacent
26. admiration
27. adolescent
28. advantage
29. advantageous
30. advertisement
31. advice
32. advisable
33. advise
34. adviser
35. affect
36. afraid
37. aggravate
38. aggressive
39. aisle
40. allot (allotting)
41. allotment
42. allowance
43. all right
44. almost
45. alphabet
46. already
47. altar
48. alter
49. although
50. all together
51. altogether
52. amateur
53. ambitious
54. American
55. among
56. amount
57. analysis

58. analyze
59. announcement
60. annual
61. answer
62. antecedent
63. anticipation
64. antidote
65. antiseptic
66. anxiety
67. apartment
68. apology
69. apparatus
70. apparently
71. appearance
72. appendicitis
73. applied
74. appointment
75. appreciation
76. approach
77. appropriate
78. approval
79. approximately
80. arctic
81. argue (arguing)
82. argument
83. aroused
84. arrangement
85. article
86. ascend
87. assistance
88. association
89. athletic
90. attack
91. attendance
92. attitude
93. attractiveness
94. audience
95. author

96. authority
97. autobiography
98. autumn
99. auxiliary
100. available
101. awkward
102. bachelor
103. balloon
104. bargain
105. basically
106. basis
107. beautiful
108. beauty
109. becoming
110. beggar
111. beginning
112. behavior
113. believing
114. beneficial
115. benefit (benefited)
116. boundary
117. breath
118. breathe
119. Britain
120. business
121. cafeteria
122. calendar
123. campaign
124. candidate
125. capital
126. career
127. careless
128. carrying
129. category
130. celebrate
131. cemetery
132. century
133. certain
134. challenge
135. changeable
136. characteristic
137. chauffeur
138. cheerfulness
139. chiefly
140. chocolate
141. choose
142. chose
143. chosen
144. circumstance
145. clothes
146. coincidence
147. column
148. comfortably
149. commercial
150. commission
151. committee
152. communication
153. community
154. companies
155. comparatively
156. comparison
157. compatible
158. compel (compelled)
159. competence
160. competition
161. completely
162. complexion
163. compliment
164. composition
165. comprehension
166. concede
167. conceivable
168. conceive
169. concentrated
170. concern
171. condemn

172. confidence
173. congratulations
174. connoisseur
175. conscience
176. conscientious
177. conscious
178. consensus
179. consequently
180. considerable
181. consistent
182. consolation
183. contemporary
184. contempt (contemptuous)
185. continually
186. continuous
187. contribution
188. controlled
189. controversy
190. convenience
191. correspondence
192. councilor
193. counselor
194. countries
195. courageous
196. courtesy
197. criticism
198. criticize
199. cruel
200. curiosity
201. curriculum
202. customary
203. customer
204. cylinder
205. dangerous
206. dealt
207. deceive
208. decidedly
209. decision
210. defenseless
211. deficiency
212. deficient
213. definite (definitely)
214. definition
215. delinquent
216. democracy
217. demonstrated
218. dependent
219. depression
220. descendant
221. descent
222. describe (description)
223. desert
224. despair
225. desperate
226. desperation
227. dessert
228. destruction
229. determination
230. detriment
231. devices
232. difference
233. difficulty
234. dilemma
235. diminish
236. dining room
237. diphtheria
238. disappear
239. disappoint
240. disastrous
241. disciple
242. discipline
243. discoveries
244. discrimination
245. discuss
246. disease
247. dissatisfied

248. dissipate
249. distinguished
250. divide
251. divine
252. doctor
253. doesn't
254. dominant
255. dormitories
256. drunkenness
257. ecstasy
258. edition
259. education
260. effect
261. efficiency
262. efficient
263. eighth
264. eighty
265. either
266. elementary
267. eligible
268. eliminate
269. eloquently
270. embarrass
271. emergency
272. emigrate
273. eminent
274. emperor
275. emphasize
276. emptiness
277. encouragement
278. enemies
279. English
280. enormous
281. enough
282. enterprise
283. entertainment
284. enthusiasm
285. entirely
286. entrance
287. environment
288. equally
289. equipment
290. equipped
291. equivalent
292. escape
293. especially
294. essential
295. eventually
296. everybody
297. evidently
298. exaggerating
299. exceed
300. excellent
301. except
302. exceptionally
303. excess
304. excitable
305. exercise
306. exhausted
307. exhibit
308. exhilarate
309. existence
310. expectation
311. expenses
312. experience
313. experiment
314. explanation
315. extravagant
316. facilities
317. faithfulness
318. fallacy
319. familiar
320. families
321. fantasy
322. fascinating
323. favorite

324. feasible
325. February
326. fictitious
327. finally
328. financially
329. financier
330. foreign
331. foreword
332. formally
333. formerly
334. forty
335. forward
336. foundation
337. fourteen
338. fourth
339. fraternity
340. friendliness
341. fulfill
342. fundamental
343. funeral
344. furniture
345. further
346. gaiety
347. gauge
348. genius
349. gentleman
350. genuine
351. glorious
352. goggles
353. gorgeous
354. government
355. governor
356. grammar
357. grandeur
358. grievous
359. guarantee
360. guidance
361. handicapped

362. handkerchief
363. happening
364. happiness
365. harass
366. haughtiness
367. healthy
368. hear
369. heartily
370. heavier
371. height
372. helpful
373. here
374. heroes
375. heroines
376. hindrance
377. hopelessness
378. hoping
379. hospitality
380. huge
381. humiliate
382. humorous
383. hungry
384. hurriedly
385. hygiene
386. hypocrisy
387. hypocrite
388. ignorance
389. imaginary
390. imagine
391. immediately
392. immense
393. immigrant
394. impassable
395. important
396. impossible
397. inadequate
398. inauguration
399. incidentally

400. increase
401. incredible
402. indefinitely
403. independent
404. indictment
405. indispensable
406. individual
407. industrial
408. influence
409. influential
410. ingenious
411. initiative
412. innocence
413. insistence
414. installation
415. instructor
416. instrument
417. intellectual
418. intelligent
419. interest (interesting)
420. interference
421. interpretation
422. interruption
423. intolerance
424. introductory
425. invariable
426. involved
427. irrelevant
428. irresistible
429. irritable
430. island
431. its
432. it's
433. January
434. jealousy
435. jewelry
436. kindergarten
437. knowledge

438. labeled
439. laboratory
440. laboriously
441. language
442. leisurely
443. lengthening
444. libraries
445. license
446. lieutenant
447. lightening
448. lightning
449. likelihood
450. literature
451. liveliest
452. livelihood
453. liveliness
454. loneliness
455. lose (losing)
456. lovable
457. loyalty
458. luxuries
459. magazine
460. magnificent
461. maintenance
462. management
463. managing
464. maneuver
465. manufacturing
466. marriage
467. marriageable
468. material
469. mathematics
470. meanness
471. meant
472. mechanics
473. medicine
474. mentality
475. merchandise

476. metropolitan
477. millionaire
478. miniature
479. miscellaneous
480. mischief
481. mischievous
482. misspelled
483. modified
484. monotonous
485. month
486. moral
487. morale
488. mosquitoes
489. multiplication
490. muscle
491. musician
492. mysterious
493. narrative
494. nationalities
495. naturally
496. necessary
497. negative
498. Negro
499. Negroes
500. neighbor
501. neither
502. Niagara
503. niece
504. nineteen
505. ninety
506. ninth
507. noticeable
508. noticing
509. numerous
510. obstacle
511. occasion (occasionally)
512. occupying
513. occur (occurred)

514. occurrence
515. occurring
516. o'clock
517. omission
518. omit
519. omitted
520. operate
521. operation
522. opinion
523. opponent
524. opportunities
525. oppose
526. optimism
527. optimistic
528. organization
529. origin
530. originally
531. overwhelming
532. paid
533. pamphlet
534. pandemonium
535. pantomime
536. parallel
537. paralyze
538. participated
539. particularly
540. partner
541. passed
542. past
543. pastime
544. peace
545. peaceable
546. peculiarities
547. penniless
548. perceive
549. performance
550. permanent
551. permissible

552. permit
553. perseverance
554. persistent
555. personal
556. personnel
557. perspiration
558. persuade
559. pertain
560. phase
561. phenomenon
562. Philippines
563. philosophy
564. physical
565. physician
566. picnicking
567. piece
568. planned
569. planning
570. plausible
571. playwright
572. pleasant
573. politician
574. portrayed
575. possessions
576. possibility
577. possible
578. poverty
579. practically
580. prairie
581. precedent
582. preceding
583. predominant
584. prefer
585. preferable
586. preference
587. preferred
588. prejudice
589. preparation

590. prepare
591. prescription
592. presence
593. prevalence
594. previous
595. primitive
596. principal
597. principle
598. privilege
599. probably
600. procedure
601. proceed
602. process
603. professor
604. prominent
605. pronounce
606. pronunciation
607. propaganda
608. proprietor
609. provisions
610. psychology
611. punctuation
612. pursue
613. qualities
614. quantity
615. quarter
616. questionnaire
617. quiet
618. realize
619. really
620. receipt
621. receivable
622. receive
623. recognition
624. recognize
625. recollection
626. recommend (recom-
   mendation)

627. reference
628. referred
629. refrigerator
630. regard
631. regrettable
632. relative
633. relevant
634. relieve
635. religion
636. religious
637. remember
638. remembrance
639. reminisce
640. renowned
641. repentance
642. repetition
643. representative
644. requirements
645. research
646. resources
647. response
648. responsibility
649. restaurant
650. reverend
651. reverent
652. reviewing
653. rhythm
654. ridicule
655. ridiculous
656. righteous
657. rivalry
658. roommate
659. sacrifice
660. safety
661. sandwich
662. satirical
663. satisfaction
664. satisfied

665. Saturday
666. saucer
667. sausage
668. scarcity
669. scene
670. scenery
671. schedule
672. scheme
673. scholarship
674. scientific
675. secretary
676. seize
677. selection
678. semester
679. sentence
680. separate
681. seriousness
682. several
683. severely
684. shepherd
685. shining
686. shoulder
687. shriek
688. siege
689. significance
690. similar
691. sincerely
692. situation
693. solution
694. sophomore
695. sorrowful
696. source
697. sovereignty
698. specialization
699. specifically
700. specimen
701. spectacle
702. speech

703. sponsor
704. statement
705. stationary
706. stationery
707. stenographer
708. stopping
709. straighten
710. strength
711. strenuous
712. stubborn
713. studied
714. studying
715. subscription
716. substantiate
717. substitute
718. subtle
719. succeeding
720. successful
721. suddenness
722. sufficient
723. summarize
724. summary
725. superintendent
726. supersede
727. superstitious
728. supervisor
729. suppose
730. suppress
731. surprise
732. surrounded
733. susceptible
734. suspense
735. suspicious
736. swimming
737. syllable
738. symbol
739. symmetrical
740. synonymous
741. system
742. tactfulness
743. technical
744. technique
745. temperament
746. temperate
747. temperature
748. temporarily
749. tenant
750. tendency
751. tenement
752. territory
753. than
754. their
755. then
756. theories
757. therefore
758. they're
759. thirtieth
760. thirty
761. thoroughly
762. thought
763. thousand
764. to
765. together
766. tomorrow
767. too
768. tradition
769. tragedy
770. transferred
771. transportation
772. tremendous
773. trespass
774. truly
775. try (tried)
776. Tuesday
777. twelfth
778. twentieth

779. two
780. typical
781. tyranny
782. unanimous
783. unbelievable
784. uncivilized
785. unconscious
786. uncontrollable
787. undesirable
788. undoubtedly
789. uneasiness
790. unforgettable
791. universities
792. unmanageable
793. unnecessary
794. until
795. unusual
796. usage
797. useful
798. usual
799. usually
800. vacuum
801. valleys
802. valuable
803. varieties
804. various
805. vaudeville
806. vegetable
807. vengeance
808. ventilate
809. verbatim
810. vernacular
811. versatile
812. veteran
813. vicinity
814. victim
815. view
816. village
817. villain
818. villainous
819. vinegar
820. virtuous
821. visible
822. vitamin
823. volume
824. waive
825. wander
826. warranted
827. wave
828. wealthiest
829. weather
830. Wednesday
831. weird
832. whenever
833. where
834. wherever
835. whether
836. whole
837. wholesale
838. wholly
839. whose
840. wintry
841. withal
842. withholding
843. witnessed
844. wonder
845. wonderful
846. wrench
847. writing
848. written
849. yacht
850. Yankee
851. Yiddish
852. yield
853. your
854. you're

855. yourself	858. zero
856. zealot	859. zigzag
857. zenith	860. zinc

Quite likely, this list of 860 words does not contain some of those that give you the most trouble. Now would be an excellent time to start your own list of "spelling demons."

18

TWENTY-FIVE TROUBLESOME
BEGINNINGS AND ENDINGS

The preceding chapters of this little book have treated every major and minor approach to better spelling that has ever been sensibly attempted. There remain, however, a few trouble spots that cannot neatly be tucked into any of the earlier chapters. Several of the comments and recommendations that follow have been briefly touched on but deserve fuller treatment.

1. ac-, acc-.
   Numerous everyday words begin with *ac-*:

ace	acid	acne
ache	academic	acquire
acrid	action	active

acc- is the correct spelling when what follows is *l, o, r,* or *u:*

acclimate	accomplish	accrue
accuse	accompany	account
accustom	accredit	

Note these exceptions: *acorn, across, acute.* Words like *accident* and *accede* cause no trouble because each *c* is separately pronounced.

2. -acious, -aceous, -atious.
   These troublesome endings are pronounced the same, but by far the most common spelling is *-acious:*

gracious	audacious	pugnacious

When in doubt, use *-acious*. Only a few words end in *-aceous* and
-atious:

curvaceous	herbaceous	sebaceous
vexatious	flirtatious	ostentatious

3. af-, aff-.
   When *a* is the prefix of a word beginning with *f, af-* is,
   of course, the correct usage:

afield	afire	afresh
afloat	aflutter	afoot

Also beginning with *-af* are such words as *Africa* and *afraid.*
Before a vowel or the consonants *l* and *r, aff-* is the accepted
spelling:

affable	affect	affidavit
afford	affront	affluent

4. ag-, agg-.
   When it is a prefix to a full word, *ag-* is the standard
   spelling:

aglow	aglitter	agleam

Ag- is also correct when it precedes *r* in certain words:

aground	agree	agrarian
agriculture	agronomy	agreement

The following words begin with *agg-:*

aggressive	aggregate	agglomerate
aggravate	aggrandize	aggrieved

5. al-, all-.
   Visual memory is about your only help in spelling
   words with these beginnings. The following common
   words begin with *all-:*

allergy	allowance	allege
alloy	alligator	alleviate
allot	ally	allocate

Words beginning with *al-* are quite numerous:

almanac	aloft	aloof
almost	aloe	altogether
almighty	alone	aloft
alimony	along	alphabet

6. ap-, app-.
   Don't omit the second *p* in words like these:

apply	appoint	apparent
appear	approach	apparel
apparatus	approve	appeal
approximate	application	appetite

Ap- words are even more numerous than those beginning with *app-*:

apartment	apart	aphorism
apology	apathy	apiece
apostrophe	ape	aplomb
aperture	apex	apoplexy
apostate	apostle	apothecary

7. -ard, -ards.
   In words like *backward* and *upward*, the ending without *s* (*-ard*) is the adjective form (a *backward* step, an *upward* movement). As an adverb, such a word may be spelled with or without an *s*; walking *backward* or *backwards*. The following words are all spelled correctly:

downward, downwards	toward, towards
forward, forwards	homeward, homewards

Recommendation: Use the spelling without *s* wherever possible since it is shorter.

8. -ayed, -aid.
   Some verbs ending in *-ay* form their past tense by
   adding *-ed:*

   play, played   betray, betrayed pray, prayed

But the past tenses of most verbs ending in *-ay* are formed
with *-aid:*

   pay, paid   outlay, outlaid   say, said
   lay, laid   mislay, mislaid   waylay, waylaid

9. col-, coll-.
   Before any vowel, *coll-* is more frequently correct than
   col-:

   collar   collect   collide
   collapse   college   collaborate
   collie   collusion   collier
   colloquy   colloquial   collateral

A somewhat smaller number of words begin with *col-*, among
them:

   colony   colonize   color
   cologne   colonel   colossal
   coliseum   colic   colon

10. com-, comm-.
    Only memory and luck will help you to distinguish be-
    tween these spellings. But one fact will help: many
    more words begin with *comm-* than with *com-:*

    comedy   coma   comity
    comet   comic   comestible
    comatose   comedian   coming

    command   commemorate   commend
    commencement   comma   comment
    commander   commercial   commission
    commit   commune   committee
    commentary   commiserate   commodore
    common   communism   communicate

11. con-, conn-.
    Before a vowel, the following are the only words of
    consequence spelled with *con-*:

| cone | conical | conifer |
| conic | conundrum | coniferous |

If a vowel does not follow this beginning, numerous words
are spelled with *con-*:

concert	concern	concentrate
conception	concrete	conclude
confirm	confident	conflict
congregation	conquest	consent

If you are in doubt, double the *n* when the next letter is a
vowel:

connect	connive	connective
connate	connivance	connoisseur
connote	connotation	connubial

12. cor-, corr-.
    Before a vowel, *corr-* is more common than *cor-*:

correct	corridor	correlate
correspond	corrupt	corrosive
corrugate	corroborate	corrode
correctitude	correlative	corruption

The only *cor-* words that might be misspelled are:

coral	coronary	corollary
coronation	coroner	corespondent
cornice	cornucopia	corona

13. -cy, -sy.
    When in doubt about ending a word having this
    sound, choose *-cy:*

fluency	lunacy	consistency
legacy	literacy	regency
infancy	frequency	sufficiency
constancy	democracy	secrecy

Note, however, that the *-sy* ending is needed in some words:

jealousy	hypocrisy	heresy
idiosyncrasy	pleurisy	ecstasy

14. dis-, diss-.
The addition of the prefix *dis-* to a word or word root beginning with *s* produces a "double *s*" pattern:

dissatisfy	dissident	disseminate
dissipate	dissimilar	dissociate
dissolve	dissonance	dissent
dissuade	dissolution	dissect

The addition of *dis-* to a word beginning with any letter other than *s* requires only one *s:*

disagree	disapprove	dispute
disappoint	displeasure	disqualify
disconnect	disprove	disquiet

15. -el, -ell.
One-syllable words end in *ell:*

tell	shell	well
bell	hell	fell
dell	sell	jell

Words of two or more syllables normally end in *-el:*

compel	rebel	excel
dispel	propel	expel
impel	repel	lapel
jewel	travel	parallel

16. en-, in-.
Numerous English words start with the prefix *en-* or *in-* with no change in meaning. In these words, *en-* is preferred:

enrich	enchant	encounter
endorse	enthrone	enclose
endure	entitle	enclosure
entrap	enfold	encase
engulf	entrust	entomb

In the following words *in-* is preferred:

inquiry	ingrain	insurance
indoctrinate	insure	invoke
incorporate	infiltrate	inure

17. -ence, -ense.

Most words of more than one syllable end in *-ence* rather than *-ense:*

consequence	difference	experience
independence	sequence	affluence
impatience	eloquence	influence

Words ending in *-ense* include:

nonsense	defense	pretense
intense	condense	offense

18. -ension, -ention.

When faced with a choice between *-ension* and *-ention,* try to think of another form of the word being spelled. An *s* in that form suggests *-ension* (tense—tension), although exceptions are numerous. If the preceding letter is *h,* the ending is always *-ension* (apprehend—apprehension). If the preceding letter is *t,* the ending should be *-ention:*

comprehension	contention
tension	convention
suspension	distention
condescension	prevention
extension	retention
pretension	circumvention
dissension	intention

19. -eys, -ies, -ys.
    Nouns that end in *ey* are usually pluralized by adding *s:*

alley—alleys	attorney—	monkey—monkeys
valley—valleys	attorneys	
key—keys	donkey—donkeys	

Nouns that end in *y* preceded by a consonant are pluralized by changing *y* to *i* and adding *es:*

sky—skies	dairy—dairies	diary—diaries
fly—flies	spy—spies	delivery—deliveries
lady—ladies	soliloquy—	
story—stories	soliloquies	

If a proper noun ends in *y*, form the plural by adding *s:*

Harry—Harrys	Judy—Judys	Dorothy—Dorothys
Jerry—Jerrys	Mary—Marys	
Sally—Sallys		

20. fore-, for-.
    With one exception, *fore-* as the initial spelling of a word indicates a meaning of "before," or "earlier," or "front," or "previous," or "the front part of":

forearm	foreword	forehead
foretold	foreman	foreground
forecast	forefinger	forefather
forewoman	foremost	forenoon

The one exception is *foreclose* (*foreclosure*), which has none of the meanings mentioned.

Other words in which the prefix does not have any meaning of "early" or "before" or the like are spelled with *for-:*

forget	forward	forlorn
forgive	forbid	forbear
forsake	forfeit	forbearance
forgiveness	forgo	format

21. -k to -c.

A verb ending in -*oke* has noun and adjective forms in which the *k* changes to *c* before the vowel *a:*

convoke—convocation—convocable
invoke—invocation—invocatory
provoke—provocation—provocative
evoke—evocation—evocative
revoke—revocation—irrevocable

22. -ment.

This suffix is added directly to a verb to form a noun:

develop—development   embarrass—embarrassment
equip—equipment   endanger—endangerment
assign—assignment   assess—assessment

Verbs ending in *e* form nouns without adding an additional *e:*

manage—management   place—placement
entangle—entanglement   arrange—arrangement
amuse—amusement   state—statement

An often misspelled exception is "argue—argument." Also, with verbs ending in -*dge* (judge, lodge, etc.) the preferred spelling drops the final *e:* judgment, lodgment.

23. mis-, miss-.

The prefix *mis-* provides a negative force to a word:

conduct—misconduct   behave—misbehave
place—misplace   understand—misunderstand
apply—misapply   cast—miscast

When *mis-* is prefix to a word that starts with *s*, a double *s* occurs:

shape—misshape   step—misstep
spell—misspell   speak—misspeak
state—misstate   spend—misspend

24. -ope, -oap.
    Soap is the only common word ending in *-oap*. Other words with this sound end in *-ope:*

antelope	scope	grope
mope	slope	dope
elope	hope	rope

25. -uous.
    Don't omit the first *u* in the endings of these words:

arduous	virtuous	innocuous
strenuous	conspicuous	unctuous
superfluous	impetuous	continuous
contemptuous	tempestuous	ingenuous

19

TEST YOURSELF: THIRTY-FIVE
GAMES AND QUIZZES

1. Insert *ei* or *ie* in the following:

ach ____ ve	n ____ ther
bel ____ f	p ____ ce
br ____ f	perc ____ ve
c ____ ling	rec ____ pt
conc ____ t	rel ____ ve
dec ____ ve	rev ____ w
for ____ gn	sh ____ ld
financ ____ r	shr ____ k
misch ____ vous	v ____ l
n ____ ghbor	y ____ ld

2. Insert *ei* or *ie* in the following:

cash ____ r	rec ____ ve
ch ____ f	retr ____ ve
f ____ ld	s ____ zure
fr ____ ght	sh ____ k
h ____ nous	st ____ n
h ____ r	surv ____ llance
h ____ ght	th ____ f
l ____ sure	v ____ n
p ____ r	w ____ ght
pr ____ st	w ____ rd

3. Add *-ed* and *-ing* to the following:

array	imply	rely
copy	marry	reply
dally	pay	say
delay	pity	stay
deny	pray	toy
destroy	pry	try
empty	rally	typify

4. Add *-ness* to each of the following:

bare	icy	pretty
busy	lively	shy
empty	lovely	wry
happy		

5. *Study—studies—studied—studying.* Supply the same verb forms for each of the following:

bury	enjoy	pity
carry	envy	pray
cry	marry	stay
dignify		

6. Add *-ing* and *-ment* to each of the following:

abridge	atone	judge
acknowledge	argue	move
advise	excite	settle
amuse		

7. Add *-ed* and *-ing* to each of the following:

acquit	occur	tax
admit	prefer	transfer
control	refer	transmit
infer		

8. The prefix *mis-* means "bad" or "wrong." It is found in many words such as *mistake, misnomer, misadvise, misinformation, mispronunciation, misrepresent, mis-*

gauge, misadventure, misbelief, etc. First, write as
many words as you can recall beginning with each of
the following prefixes. Then expand your lists by reference to a good dictionary:

ad-	non-	pro-
de-	ob-	sub-
hyper-	poly-	ultra-
inter-		

9. By means of a suffix (*-ible* or *-able,* *-ly* or *-ally,* *-ence* or
   -ance, -ion, etc.) form an adjective, adverb, or noun
   from each of the following words. Example: *admire: ad-
   mirable, admirably, admiration.* Not all these parts of
   speech can be formed from each word, but one or more
   can be:

accept	describe	love
advertise	detect	notice
allow	discern	remark
deduce		

10. Add *-ed* and either *-able* or *-ible* to the following:

avail	excite	reverse
comprehend	like	suggest
depend	presume	value
dismiss		

11. Add *-ally* or *-ly* to each of the following:

accident	incredible	occasion
complete	intention	physic
entire	lyric	true
incident		

12. From many verbs nouns may be formed which end in
    -ance, -ence; -ar, -er, -or; -ary, -ery. Example: *contrib-
    ute, contributor.* Form a noun from each of the
    following words:

act	defer	protect
adhere	defy	provide
beg	distill (distil)	repent
carry	lecture	station
collect	lie	subsist
confer	occur	visit
counsel	prefer	

13. Form plurals of each of the following:

apparatus	bus	dynamo
area	cross	elf
billiards	examination	hoof
bureau	dwarf	measles
metropolis	synopsis	thief
poet laureate	tactics	torpedo
quota		

14. Some compounds are spelled as one word (*football*), some as hyphenated words (*four-dimensional*), some as two words (*reading desk*). Indicate the correct spelling of:

airtight	helterskelter	runin
boobytrap	highschool	schoolboy
campfire	inspite	selfstarter
chickenhearted	laborsaving	sodawater
downstairs	offstage	sunrise
drawbridge	pitchdark	twentyfour
hangeron	quietspoken	

15. Supply the missing letter in each of the following:

ab _____ ence	excell _____ nt
absor _____ tion	exigen _____ y
apol _____ gy	han _____ kerchief
Ba _____ tist	iden _____ ity
caf _____ teria	min _____ ature
calend _____ r	opt _____ mistic
cem _____ tery	sacr _____ legious
compar _____ tive	sep _____ rate
disinfect _____ nt	sim _____ lar
dorm _____ tory	temper _____ ment

16. Supply the missing letter in each of the following:

appar _____ nt	nes _____ le
cors _____ ge	priv _____ lege
crim _____ nal	p _____ rsue
def _____ nite	r _____ diculous
friv _____ lous	sacr _____ fice
gramm _____ r	su _____ prise
ignor _____ nt	tra _____ edy
instruct _____ r	tres _____ le
irresist _____ ble	vulg _____ r
livel _____ hood	We _____ nesday

17. Some of the following words are correctly spelled, some incorrectly. Indicate which ones are which.

atheletic	height	reccommend
competition	mischieveous	safty
desireable	naturally	sulphur
discipline	obstacal	suppress
dissappointed	occassion	vengeance
embarassed	outragous	villain
environment	perseverance	

18. Which of the following are correctly spelled, which incorrectly?

alright	appelation	commited
analogous	changable	conscientious

Continue to indicate which of the following are correctly spelled, which incorrectly.

developement	paralel	scurrulous
ecstasy	pidgeon	symetrical
innoculate	questionaire	temperature
occasionally	renege	tendency
pantomime	rythmical	

19. Which of the following proper names are correctly spelled, which incorrectly?

Americian	Hawaian	Saturday
Britian	Kruschev	Tennesee
Brughel	Louisiana	Tripali
Burma	Massachusetts	Uraguay
Conneticut	Oragon	Wisconson
Edinburg	Phillipines	Worcestershire
February	Rockerfeller	

20. Consult your dictionary for the preferred or variant spellings of:

analyze	center	fulfil
armor	defense	instalment
canyon	dialogue	judgment
catalogue	esthetic	medieval
monologue	sulphur	traveler
savior	theatre	vigor
sextet	tranquillity	

21. The combining form *graph* appears in many English words. It comes from the Greek *graphos* (*graphein*, "to write"). Two examples are *telegraph*, "writing from a distance," and *monograph*, "writing on a single subject." Make a list of as many words as you can think of, or find in your dictionary, containing *graph* as a combining form.

22. The following is a list of everyday words with pronunciations as shown in reliable dictionaries. Spell each of them correctly:

WEBSTER'S NEW COLLEGIATE DICTIONARY	WEBSTER'S NEW WORLD DICTIONARY
ă • pēl′	ə-pēl′
bĭz′nĕs	biz′nis
drī	drī
ĕk • sĕl′	ik-sel′
kăl′ĕn • dēr	kal′ən-dēr
kōld	kōld

nĕs′ĕ • sĕr′ĭ   nes′ə-ser′i

ôr′ĕnj   ôr′ənj

prồ • pōz′   prə • pōz′

thûr′ồ   thûr′ō

23. Whether a good or bad speller, you will need to consult your dictionary frequently. You will lose time by not knowing the alphabet so thoroughly that you do not have to hesitate. Arrange the following words in the order in which they appear in a dictionary.

jump	running
jean	risk
jilt	race
jerk	round
jiffy	jelly
jeer	jeep
juvenile	join
radio	rainfall
read	remain
refine	red

24. Determine whether a study of the derivations of the following words will aid you in spelling them correctly:

absence	judicial
assign	language
bilious	mathematical
catercorner	pasteurize
criticism	possess
descend	research
emerald	ridiculous
foreign	shoulder
halitosis	typical
instrument	Wednesday

25. Using directions given in Exercise 21, list as many words as you can containing each of these combining forms:

electro-   phon-
forma-   -phone
para-   -ward

26. Correctly place apostrophes (only where needed) in
the following:

   My mother-in-laws room
   My 5s are legible; yours look like ss.
   Hasnt he forgotten the troops uniforms?
   "Its theirs, not ours," Jack replied.
   He prefers Sophocles plays to Marxs tracts.
   King Edward VIIIs operation
   Thats somebody elses work, not hers.
   World War II (1939–45)
   Whos going to whose party tonight?
   You use too many *could bes* and *maybes*.

27. Which word in each of the following pairs of words is
spelled correctly? Find on pages 133–142 the spelling
rule which applies.

   achieve *or* acheive   carries *or* carrys
   unnamed *or* unamed   fortieth *or* fortyeth
   replacable *or* replaceable thief *or* theif
   amusement *or* amusment   mimicking *or* mimicing
   photostatted *or* photo-   guideance *or* guidance
   stated

28. Using suggestions given on pages 150–154, devise a
mnemonic for each of the *ten* words which give you
the greatest spelling difficulty. Don't strain, but also
don't worry if a mnemonic is quite bizarre: it's for your
use only.

29. As pointed out several times in this book, studying
lists of words difficult to spell is not really helpful.
First, the only useful lists are of words which trouble
you yourself. Second, most lists of "demons" contain
words which are rarely used and which would stop
even excellent spellers.

Here is a list of seventy-five troublesome words, most or all of which you might use. Choose the correct (or preferred) spelling from the two columns. A score of sixty or more qualifies you as a superior speller.

1. absence	abscence
2. accidently	accidentally •
3. accomodate °	accommodate
4. acheive	achieve °
5. acknowledgment•	acknowledgement
6. acquaintance	aquaintance•
7. allotted ↵	alloted
8. analize	analyze ↄ
9. anoint°	annoint
10. arguement	argument•
11. assistant ↗	assisstant
12. bankruptcy •	bankrupcy
13. basically•	basicly
14. benefited ↙	benefitted
15. changable •	changeable
16. commission ↙	commision
17. commitee↴	committee
18. connoiseur ↙	connoisseur
19. conscientious •	conscientous
20. defenseless	defenceless↗
21. dilettante	dilletante ↄ
22. disappoint	disapoint •
23. disasterous	disastrous ↙
24. dissatisfied	disatisfied•
25. dissipate	disippate •
26. drunkenness	drunkeness ↙
27. embarrassment	embarassment ↗
28. encouragment ↙	encouragement
29. exhiliration •	exhilaration
30. familiar	familar ↙
31. fascinating ↙	facinating
32. Febuary	February↙
33. genealogy	geneology ↙

34.	goverment	government
35.	harrass	harass
36.	hypocrisy	hypocricy
37.	incidently	incidentally
38.	innoculate	inoculate
39.	iridescent	irridescent
40.	labortory	laboratory
41.	leisurely	liesurely
42.	loneliness	lonliness
43.	neice	niece
44.	nineth	ninth
45.	noticeable	noticable
46.	occurence	occurrence
47.	optomistic	optimistic
48.	pamphlet	pamplet
49.	permissable	permissible
50.	picnicking	picnicing
51.	practicly	practically
52.	preparation	preperation
53.	pronunciation	pronounciation
54.	puntuation	punctuation
55.	recommend	reccomend
56.	restaurant	restarant
57.	scarsity	scarcity
58.	seize	sieze
59.	siege	seige
60.	superstiton	superstition
61.	supprised	surprised
62.	temperament	temperment
63.	tradegy	tragedy
64.	truly	truely
65.	tyrany	tyranny
66.	ukelele	ukulele
67.	unforgetable	unforgettable
68.	unnecessary	unecessary
69.	vacilate	vacillate
70.	villianous	villainous
71.	Wednesday	Wensday

72.	weight	wieght
73.	weird	wierd
74.	wield	weild
75.	yeild	yield

30. You are an above-average speller if you can score 75 or more on the following list of 100 words, which range from "trouble makers" to outright "demons." Master them. Then try them on your friends—and your enemies.

1. academy	29. exercise	57. orchid
2. accessory	30. facile	58. overrun
3. accumulate	31. fascinate	59. paralysis
4. acoustics	32. frantically	60. perennial
5. alimentary	33. fulfilled	61. pharmaceutical
6. aloha	34. garage	62. phosphorus
7. anonymity	35. *Gesundheit*	63. phrenology
8. apparatus	36. gnome	64. phylactery
9. attendant	37. haughty	65. poinsettia
10. avoirdupois	38. hearse	66. precinct
11. baccalaureate	39. homogeneous	67. pseudo
12. bullion	40. impromptu	68. psychiatry
13. buoy	41. innuendo	69. queue
14. bureaucracy	42. irreducible	70. quinine
15. cantankerous	43. irrelevant	71. rarefied
16. catechism	44. jeopardize	72. rehearsal
17. collaborate	45. knapsack	73. rendezvous
18. consensus	46. labyrinth	74. reservoir
19. corollary	47. larynx	75. rheumatic
20. dahlia	48. licorice	76. saxophone
21. defendant	49. liqueur	77. schedule
22. desiccated	50. mediocre	78. seismograph
23. dilapidated	51. millennium	79. separation
24. disastrous	52. moratorium	80. sieve
25. eleemosynary	53. naphtha	81. silhouette
26. emphatically	54. negotiable	82. spontaneity
27. eulogy	55. notarize	83. surveillance
28. exaggerate	56. octogenarian	84. thermometer

85. tonsillitis	91. vice versa	97. xylophone
86. tranquil	92. vitamin	98. yeast
87. turgid	93. vulnerable	99. zinnia
88. ultimatum	94. wharf	100. zoological
89. umbrella	95. wiener	
90. uterus	96. wrestle	

31. Fix in your mind the spelling of these medical terms by discovering how they are formed with the aid of combining forms, prefixes, and suffixes:

anesthesiology	ophthalmology
cardiovascular	orthopedics
endocrinology	otolaryngology
gastroenterology	pathology
hematology	pediatrics
neurology	psychiatry
obstetrics	radiology
oncology	urology

32. The game Doublets is played by altering one word into another through changing one letter at a time, each step resulting in a new word. Here's how to change *four* to *five:*

four—foul—fool—foot—fort—fore—fire—five

Change each of the following:

chin into *nose*	*poor* into *rich*
tears into *smile*	*winter* into *summer*

33. Choose the correctly spelled word in each of the following pairs:

absurd—abserd	dependant—dependent
across—acros	develope—develop
alright—all right	existence—existance
condemn—condem	humorous—humerous
convenient—convenent	occassion—occasion
criticise—criticize	omitted—omited
daily—daley	lonliness—loneliness

remittance—remitance   tacitun—taciturn
resistable—resistible   tolorate—tolerate
separate—seperate   woolen—woollen

34. Here is a list of words, some of them relatively new, that are being increasingly used. Fix their meanings and their spellings so as to be up-to-date in your word usage.

aerobic	fusion	quantum
algorithm	gentrification	quark
astrodome	geodesis	quasar
astrophysics	helix	replication
bioelectricity	heterodynamics	retrovirus
cellulose	hydrospace	rodenticide
cloning	laser	semiconductor
cognitive	mach	silicon
cryogenics	microwave	subatomic
diabetologist	oceanography	supernova
dioxin	ordnance	theodolite
electronics	polymer	ultrasound
extraterrestrial	pseudopods	unicellular

35. In each group of three words below, one may be misspelled. Find the misspelled word; then decide which rule, if any, applies to it. In the space at the left, write a letter to indicate that the correct spelling of the word falls under the rule treating: a—*ei* or *ie*, according to preceding letter and pronunciation of the vowels; b—final *e* or final *y* when a suffix is added; c—doubling the final consonant (or not) when a suffix is added; d—exceptional spelling required to preserve the pronunciation of the word; e—none of these: the correct spelling of the word is contrary to rule.

1. conceive   2. neighbor
   drooping   benefited
   changable   sieze

3. briefing
   writing
   layed
4. beleiving
   looted
   lovable
5. annoyance
   alloted
   extremely
6. likelyhood
   weighing
   fighting
7. grievous
   forgetable
   happiness
8. kercheif
   reference
   meanness
9. canceled
   noticable
   luckily
10. leaving
   ladylike
   developed

GLOSSARY:

TERMS USED IN THIS BOOK

Any useful book on spelling must use expressions that may be unfamiliar to you but are closely tied to the spelling problem. Below you will find brief definitions or explanations of several linguistic terms. Some of these are fully defined in the book itself; others are used or implied. When studying the book itself, refer to this glossary if you come across an expression that you do not fully understand. An effort has been made to include all terms likely to need clarification. If you are still in doubt, consult your dictionary.

accent: Accent is the emphasis given to a letter or syllable or word when speaking it. This increased force results from stress, or pitch, or both. In dictionaries, marks are used to show the placing and kind of emphasis required. For example, in the word *envelop* the second syllable is accented: en vel' op. In *envelope*, the first syllable has primary stress, or accent: en' vel ope. See *stress*, below.

adjective: An adjective modifies a noun or pronoun by describing, limiting, or in some other closely related way making meaning more nearly exact. An adjective may indicate quality or quantity, may identify or set limits. Adjectives are therefore of three general types: descriptive (a *red* hat, a *hard* lesson, a *damaged* thumb); limiting (the *fourth* period, her *former* home, *many* times); proper (an *American* play, a *Colorado* melon).

Some adjectives—indeed, most—have endings that mark them as adjectives. The more important of these include:

-y: rocky, funny, dreamy, fussy, muddy
-ful: harmful, faithful, hurtful, sinful
-less: stainless, timeless, lawless, guiltless
-en: golden, wooden, given, hidden, rotten
-able (*-ible*): favorable, desirable, credible
-ive: obtrusive, submissive, impulsive
-ous: amorous, ridiculous, generous, marvelous
-ish: womanish, selfish, Danish, fortyish
-al: cordial, optional, experimental, judicial
-ic: metric, philosophic, authentic, artistic
-ary: primary, visionary, contrary, secondary
-some: meddlesome, tiresome, handsome, troublesome

An adjective may modify a noun directly ("this *yellow* light thrown upon the color of his ambitions") or indirectly ("the survivors, *weary* and *emaciated*, moved feebly toward the ship"). In sentences such as "The water felt *cold*" and "The corn is *ripe*," each adjective is related to the subject, the word it modifies, by a linking verb. (A linking verb has little meaning of its own; it functions primarily as a connection between subject and predicate noun or predicate adjective.) In the sentences above, *cold* and *ripe* are called *predicate adjectives* or complements.

adverb: An adverb modifies a verb, adjective, or other adverb by describing or limiting to make meaning more exact. Adverbs usually tell *how, when, where, why, how often,* or *how much.* In "A low cry came *faintly* to our ears," the adverb modifies the verb *came.* In "Close the door *very* softly," the adverb modifies the adverb *softly.*

Adverbs have the following characteristics: (1) They are commonly, but not always, distinguished from corresponding adjectives by the suffix *-ly: bad, badly; sure, surely; cold, coldly.* (2) Certain adverbs are distinguished from corresponding nouns by the suffixes *-wise* and *-ways: endways, sideways,* *lengthwise.* (3) Certain adverbs are distinguished from corresponding prepositions in not being connected to a following noun: "He ran *up*" (adverb); "he ran *up* the street" (preposition). (4) Like adjectives, but unlike nouns and verbs, adverbs may be preceded by words of the *very* group (intensifiers): "The *most exotically* dressed girl passed by"; "he went *right* by."

base word: Any word, or part of a word which is a combining form, to which may be added prefixes, suffixes, etc. Thus we refer to *mortal* as the base word, or element, of *mortality* and *cede* as the base element of the word *accede*. See *root word*, below.

capitals: Any letters written or printed in a form larger than, and often different from, that of corresponding small letters: A, B, C; a, b, c. The use of capital letters (sometimes called upper-case letters as contrasted with small, or lower-case, letters) is discussed in Chapter 13.

clause: A group of words which forms a sentence or a part of a sentence. A clause contains a subject (substantive) and a predicate (verb). "*John studied* and *I played the radio*" illustrates two separate and independent clauses. In the following sentence, the first group of italicized words is an independent clause, the second is dependent upon the first: "*I shall telephone you/when I arrive.*"

compounds: Compound words are combinations of two or more words: *doorkeeper, inasmuch as.* The use of hyphens (see below) with compound words is discussed in Chapter 12.

conjunction: A part of speech that serves as a linking or joining word to connect words or groups of words such as phrases and clauses: *and, but, for, because, since,* etc.

consonant: A consonant is a speech sound produced by restricting or stopping the breath. Consonants may be contrasted with *vowels* (see below) since the latter involve sounds made with less friction and fuller resonance. The consonants *b, d, g, k, p,* and *t* are produced by stopping and releasing the air stream.

The consonants *l, m, n,* and *r* are produced by stopping the air stream at one point while it escapes at another. In sounding the consonants *f, s, v,* and *z,* the air stream is forced through a loosely closed or narrow passage. In short, consonants are those letters (sounds) of the alphabet which are not vowels: *a, e, i, o, u.*

diacritical mark:　A mark added to a letter to indicate pronunciation by giving it a particular sound (phonetic) value or stress that distinguishes it from an unmarked letter of similar form. Thus the sound we utter in starting the alphabet may be indicated as ā, as in the words *date* and *able.* The sound of *a* in *art* and *father* is represented by ä. Every dictionary worthy of the name devotes considerable space to its own system of diacritical marks, usually running a condensed list of them on the bottom of each righthand page and a detailed explanation inside the front or back cover or in pages at the front of the dictionary. Diacritical marks are essential to correct pronunciation and thus are important in learning to spell correctly. You should become thoroughly familiar with the marks used by your dictionary.

etymology:　The branch of linguistic study that deals with the origin and development of words. For further discussion see Chapter 5.

grammar:　Grammar is ordinarily understood as a series of statements of the way a language works; English grammar is "the English way of saying things." That is, grammar concerns the form of words; their use in phrases, clauses, and sentences; their tenses, cases, and other changes in form. The word *grammar,* which comes from the Greek word *gramma* ("letter," "written symbol"), now means the structure of an entire given language.

Thus defined, grammar is unconcerned with what is "correct" or "incorrect," "right" or "wrong." However, there *is* so-called prescriptive grammar. This kind has to do with the application of "rules" as guides to expression.

homograph:　A word with the same spelling as another but with a different origin and meaning: a *bow* tie, to bend a *bow; row*, meaning "a noisy dispute" and "a straight line"; *fair*, meaning "beautiful" and also "a market"; *lead*, the metal and a word meaning "to conduct"; *air*, "atmosphere" and "a melody"; *pale*, an "enclosure" and "faintly colored." See Chapter 3 for further discussion.

homonym: A word with the same pronunciation as another but with a different origin, meaning, and sometimes spelling: *hear, here; steal, steel; meat, meet; pale, pail.* For further discussion, see Chapter 3.

hyphen: A mark used between the syllables of a divided word or the parts of a compound word. It is more a mark of spelling than of punctuation. See Chapter 12.

long sound: A pronounced vowel or consonant which is held or sounded for a relatively long time. For example, the *a* in *ape* is long; it may be held for as long as your breath lasts. In dictionaries it is marked ā. Similarly, the *e* in *easy* is long; the *i* in *mile*, etc.

morpheme: A term in linguistics for the smallest meaningful unit in an utterance. A morpheme may be a single phoneme (such as the article "a"), a prefix or suffix ("ad-," "-ism"), a single syllable or several ("girl," "instructor," "miscellaneous").

morphology: The patterns of word formation in language, including derivation and inflection. Morphology and syntax together form a basic division of grammar.

noun: A noun (derived from the Latin word *nomen*, meaning "name") designates or names a person, place, or thing; a quality, idea, or action; an event or point in time. This less than really helpful definition can be supplemented by consideration of the ways in which nouns are characterized and classified. Nouns are usually preceded by such words as *the, a, an, my, your, his, her, some, each, every, their, this, that.*

Certain nouns have characteristic endings (*-al, -tion, -ness, -ment, -ure, -dom, -ism, -ance*, for example) that distinguish them from corresponding verbs or adjectives: *arrive, arrival;*

determine, determination; depart, departure; real, realism; rely, reliance; wise, wisdom.

Nouns and identically spelled verbs may sometimes be differentiated by accent. The first member in each of these pairs of words is a noun, the second a verb: *per' mit, permit'; rec'ord, record'; sur'vey, survey'; ob' ject, object'.*

Nouns are found in set positions, such as before a verb (a *mouse* roars), after a verb (wash the *shirt*), or after a preposition (working for *money*).

Nouns may be singular or plural in number. The plural of most English nouns is obtained by adding *s* or *es* to the singular form: *girls, books, trees, fields, peaches.* Some nouns have only one form for both the singular and the plural: *deer, sheep, moose.* Some nouns have irregular plurals: *oxen, children, mice.* Some actually have no plurals: *fun, furniture.*

Nouns have three genders: (1) masculine (*man, boy*), (2) feminine (*girl, woman*), and (3) neuter (*chalk, earth*). When a noun may be either masculine or feminine, it has a common gender (*teacher, friend*).

Nouns have three cases: nominative (subject), objective, and genitive (possessive). In English, nouns have a common form for both the nominative and the objective case. An apostrophe is used to designate a noun in the genitive case: *Jack's, boat's, neighbor's.*

A *common* noun is a name given to all members of a class: *dozen, infant, farm, street, city, boy, structure.* Common nouns may be recognized as such because they do *not* begin with a capital letter (except at the beginning of a sentence or as part of a name).

A *proper* noun names a particular member of a class: it *does* begin with a capital: *Rover, Michael, Twin Cedars, Roosevelt Freeway, Atlanta, Bob Dylan, Eiffel Tower.*

An *abstract* noun is the name of a quality or general idea that cannot be known directly by the senses: *faith, happiness, courage, fear.*

Concrete nouns name material (tangible) things that can be perceived by one or more of the senses: *fire, aroma, notebook, hamburger, stone, record, cake.*

A *collective* noun names a group of individuals. Although it refers to more than one, it is singular in form: *pair, committee, squad, team, crowd, crew, assembly*.

orthography: This is a ten-dollar word to indicate what this book is all about. It means, simply, correct spelling, or spelling as a science.

particle: This is an omnibus word, a convenient catchall which includes short and indeclinable parts of speech such as articles, prepositions, conjunctions, and interjections, as well as prefixes and suffixes. These are particles: *but, oh, in, ad-, -ion*.

parts of speech: The classifications to which every word must belong: noun, pronoun, adjective, adverb, verb, preposition, conjunction, interjection. The same word may belong to several parts of speech, depending upon how it is used in a sentence.

person: The change in the form of a pronoun or verb—sometimes, merely a change in use as with verbs—to indicate whether the "person" used is the person speaking (first person), the person spoken to (second person), or the person or thing spoken about (third person): *I* read, *you* read, *he* reads.

phoneme: The smallest meaningful unit of *sound* in a language. The letters in our alphabet comprise about forty phonemes. For example, the word *wean* consists of three phonemes: *w, ē*, and *n*. Compare with *morpheme*, above.

phonetics: The branch of language study dealing with speech sounds, their production and combination, and their representation by symbols.

phrase: A group of related words not containing a subject (substantive) and predicate (verb). It may contain from two to twenty words but is always a part of a sentence and is never independent: *was running, having finished my typing, my work done, out into the cold night*, etc.

plural number: A classification of nouns, pronouns, etc., to indicate two or more units or members. *Singular* number is the classification to indicate one. For further discussion, see Chapter 10.

prefix: A syllable, group of syllables, or word united with or joined to the beginning of another word to alter its meaning or to create a new word. *Pre-* itself is a prefix in *preheat* (to heat beforehand). For further discussion, see Chapter 8.

preposition: A part of speech showing the relationship of a noun or pronoun to some other word: *at* the office, *across* the street. The word literally means "placed before": "pre-position."

pronoun: A part of speech that is used instead of a noun, primarily to avoid repetition and prevent overuse of the noun. The word *pronoun* consists of *pro*, meaning "for" or "instead of," plus *noun*.

pronunciation: The art or manner of uttering words with reference to the production of sounds, accent, etc. Pronunciation is complex and many-faceted; it involves, among other things, levels of pronunciation, dialect, provincialisms, and, most importantly, spelling. For further discussion, see Chapter 4.

root word: A base, a morpheme, to which prefixes, suffixes, etc., may be added. See *base word* and *morpheme*, above.

short sound: Sounds which are relatively brief in duration. (See *consonant* and *long sound*, above.) Many letters of the alphabet are sounded with short duration or stress and in varying degrees. Contrast the long *a* in *hate* with the short *a* in *hat*, for only one of many examples of short sounds.

sibilants: A hissing sound or the symbol for it. *S, sh, z, zh, ch,* and *j* are sibilants: *pressure, shirt, zero*, etc.

singular number: See *plural number*, above.

stress: The relative force with which a syllable is uttered. In English there are primary (strong) stress; secondary (light) stress; zero (silent) stress. See *accent*, above, and Chapter 4.

substantive: An inclusive term for a noun, pronoun, phrase or clause used as a noun, and for a verbal noun. The only practical value of the word *substantive* is that its use avoids repeating all the words used in this definition. Like most catchalls, it is a somewhat loose term.

suffix: A sound, syllable, or syllables added at the end of a word or word base to change its meaning, alter its grammatical function, or form a new word: *dark*, dark*ness*. See *prefix*, above.

syllable: A word or part of a word, usually the latter, pronounced with a single, uninterrupted sounding of the voice. Note the syllables in these words: *sec re tar y* (4 syllables); *fun ny* (2 syllables); *fa mil iar i za tion* (6 syllables).

syntax: The arrangement of words in a sentence to show their relationship. Briefly, it may be identified as *sentence structure* and is not an especially helpful term.

tense: The time of the action or of the state being expressed by the verb. The three simple, or primary, tenses are *present, past*, and *future*. The three compound, or secondary, tenses are *present perfect, past perfect, future perfect*.

verb: A part of speech expressing action or a state of being: "The river *flows*," "I *am* here."

vowel: A speech sound articulated so that there is a clear channel for the voice through the middle of the mouth. Grammatically, the vowels in English are *a, e, i, o, u* and, in some instances, *w* and *y*. See *consonant*, above.

INDEX

ABOUT THE AUTHOR

HARRY SHAW is well known as an editor, writer, lecturer, and teacher. For a number of years he was director of the Workshops in Composition at New York University and teacher of classes in advanced writing at Columbia, at both of which institutions he has done graduate work. He has worked with large groups of writers in the Washington Square Writing Center at NYU and has been a lecturer in writers' conferences at Indiana University and the University of Utah and lecturer in, and director of, the Writers' Conference in the Rocky Mountains sponsored by the University of Colorado. In 1969, Mr. Shaw was awarded the honorary degree of Doctor of Letters by Davidson College, his alma mater.

He has been managing editor and editorial director of *Look*, editor at Harper and Brothers, senior editor and vice-president of E. P. Dutton and Co., editor-in-chief of Henry Holt & Co., and director of publications for Barnes & Noble, Inc.; and also an editor at W. W. Norton & Co., Inc. He has contributed widely to many popular and scholarly national magazines and is the author or co-author of a number of books in the fields of English composition and literature, among them *Punctuate It Right!* and *Errors in English and Ways to Correct Them.*